THE NEW
Fondues

LESLEY MACKLEY

PHOTOGRAPHED BY
PATRICK McLEAVEY

PUBLISHED BY
SALAMANDER BOOKS LIMITED
LONDON

Published by Salamander Books Limited
8 Blenheim Court, Brewery Road, London N7 9NT

9 8 7 6 5 4 3 2 1

© Salamander Books Ltd., 2002

A member of the Chrysalis Group plc

ISBN 1 84065 222 5

Project managed by: Stella Caldwell
Editor: Madeline Weston
Designer: Sue Storey
Photographer: Patrick McLeavey
Photographer's Assistant: Rebecca Willis
Home Economist: Sandra Miles
Production: Phillip Chamberlain
Filmset and reproduction by: Anorax Imaging, England
Printed in Spain

CONTENTS

FOREWORD

The fondue is making a huge comeback and sales of fondue sets are rising rapidly, but you do not have to be fresh from the ski slopes to enjoy this fun and informal way of dining.

A fondue party is the perfect way to entertain. The simple preparations can be done in advance and the hostess does not need to be stuck in the kitchen but can join the guests at the table as everyone cooks their own dinner!

The New Book of Fondues is packed with over 80 recipes for fondues to suit every occasion. There are classics such as Fondue Savoyarde made with Swiss cheese, Fondue Bourgignonne and firepots from the Far East. Also included are many exciting new ideas taking their inspiration from all around the world such as Marrakesh Swordfish Fondue with fragrant North African spices, spicy Cajun Meatballs or Italian Pesto Fondue. There are also suggestions for accompaniments such as salads and sauces.

A large number of the recipes are suitable for vegetarians because they are based on cheese or vegetables, such as Pepper and Tomato Fondue or Wild Mushroom Fondue. Other recipes such as the party fondue with crudités are specifically designed to appeal to children.

Adults and children alike will be tempted by the range of sweet fondues. A pot of melted chocolate with fresh fruit for dipping is an indulgent way to end a meal and could not be simpler to prepare. Banoffee or marshmallow fondues will be popular with anyone with a sweet tooth, and as an alternative to fruit, there are recipes for simple cakes and biscuits to dip into the sweet fondues.

The New Book of Fondues also describes the different types of fondue pots available and gives plenty of advice for planning the perfect fondue party.

With *The New Book of Fondues* you are sure to find the perfect fondue to suit any occasion and any budget.

INTRODUCTION

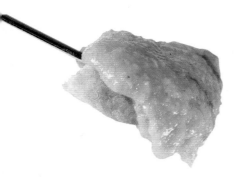

The word fondue comes from the French *fondre*, to melt. It was in the French speaking area of Switzerland that the cheese fondue originated many centuries ago. During harsh Alpine winters Swiss peasants had very limited food apart from cheese and bread, and they had few cooking utensils, so melting the cheese in one pot was a good way of using up the rather dry odds and ends of cheese.

The cheese fondue became widely known outside Switzerland when people started taking skiing holidays and enjoyed a fondue or raclette after a hard day on the slopes.

Many countries have their own version of fondue. The fondue Bourgignonne where strips of steak are cooked in hot oil is popular in France and in the Far East pieces of meat, fish or chicken are cooked in boiling stock with vegetables. At the end, noodles are added to the stock which is then served as a soup.

There are many different types of fondue sets available. A fondue set usually consists of a pot and burner with a set of four or six long-handled forks. The burner either contains a pad which has to be impregnated with methylated spirits, or a foil container of gel is placed in the burner. They will usually have a sliding cover over

Left: Large stainless steel fondue pot

Right: Cast iron fondue pot with spirit burner

the burner which will enable you to adjust the size of the flame. A cover is also usually provided for snuffing out the flame when cooking is finished. Small chocolate fondue pots have a candle to provide a gentle heat. The base containing the burner should be very stable and will need to be set on a thick mat on the table. A traditional cheese fondue pot is wide and quite shallow and usually made of earthenware or light metal such as copper. These pots are not suitable for a meat fondue as they are too open and shallow for hot oil or stock. It is quite easy to overheat the metal pots, causing the cheese to catch and burn.

A traditional meat fondue pot is taller and narrower, but most fondue pots sold nowadays tend to be this shape and they are suitable for either meat or cheese fondues. Cast iron pots tend to be the most expensive but they are the best as it is much easier to keep a steady temperature with cast iron. Another advantage is that the weight of the cast iron sets makes them more stable.

Chocolate fondues are smaller but it is not necessary to have a special pot as an attractive bowl over a night-light works well. A chocolate fondue set can also be used for keeping sauces warm at the table. Similar to a chocolate fondue set is a special pot for Bagna Cauda, and again, this is heated by a nightlight. These are usually made of terracotta.

A Mongolian hotpot or steamboat is a traditional pot for Oriental fondues. They are made of brass or aluminium and consist of a rounded pot with a funnel down the centre, set over a burner into which hot charcoal is placed. Hot stock is used and the burner keeps it bubbling throughout the meal.

Long handled forks are essential for spearing whatever is being dipped into the fondue. They usually have coloured handles or a coloured mark on the end so that each diner can identify their own fork. The food is transferred to a table fork before eating, not just for hygiene reasons, but to avoid burning - particularly

Above: Small chocolate fondue pot

important when dipping into hot oil. As an alternative to forks, bamboo skewers may be used. Little Chinese wire baskets are used with Mongolian hotpots but they are also useful for dipping meatballs, fishcakes or anything else which might be too fragile to stay on a fork.

Six is the maximum number of people who can safely and comfortably share one fondue pot, so for parties of eight or more it would be necessary to have two pots on the go. For speed, make the cheese fondue on top of the stove before transferring it to the burner. Also heat oil or stock on top of the stove and take great care when transferring the fondue pot to the burner.

CHEESE FONDUES

Choose a strongly flavoured cheese and always allow it to melt slowly. You need alcohol in a cheese fondue. Not only does it add flavour, but it lowers the boiling point and stops the protein in the cheese curdling. Do not worry if the mixture looks lumpy and separates; keep stirring and it will gradually become smooth, but do not be tempted to turn the heat up. If it becomes too thick add a little warmed

wine or cider. Encourage diners to stir the fondue right down to the bottom when they dip their bread in, this helps to keep it smooth and creamy. When the fondue is nearly finished there will be a crisp crust on the bottom off the pot. Scrape it out and divide it between the guests - it is regarded as a great treat. Use day-old bread for dipping as it will not be too crumbly and always cut the bread so that each piece has some crust on for spearing with the fork. If anybody does drop their bread in the fondue they have to perform a forfeit. Traditionally ladies have to kiss the man next to them and a man has to buy the next round of drinks!

MEAT, FISH AND SEAFOOD FONDUES

It is important to have all the ingredients and accompaniments prepared in advance. The meat should be cut and arranged attractively on plates, sauces should be prepared and served in small pots and salads should be ready to be dressed just before the cooking begins. If using oil, use a vegetable oil, but a little flavoured oil can be added if desired. The fondue pot should not be filled more than half full as the hot

oil can bubble up a bit when the meat is dipped in. The oil should be heated to 180-190C (350-375F), but if you do not have a thermometer, test it with a piece of day-old bread. A small cube will turn golden in about 30 seconds if the oil is at the correct temperature. Do not add too much food to the oil at once. This will lower the temperature of the oil and the food will not cook properly. Meat and fish should be thoroughly dried on paper towels before cooking in the hot oil, otherwise the oil will spit.

DESSERT FONDUES

Most dessert fondues are made of chocolate, but creamy fruit purées are popular too. Take great care when melting the chocolate, especially white chocolate, as it will solidify into clumps if it is overheated. Melting the chocolate with cream solves the problem. If you are dipping cake into the fondue, make sure it is not too crumbly. Day-old cake works best. If you are dipping fruit, choose firm pieces and, if possible, chill them first and the chocolate will coat them better.

— CARIBBEAN FISH FONDUE —

2 teaspoons hot pepper sauce
2 teaspoons soft brown sugar
1 teaspoon crushed allspice
1 clove garlic, crushed
½ teaspoon ground coriander
juice 1 lime
700g (1½lb) cod loin
550ml (20fl oz/2½ cups) coconut milk
1 Scotch bonnet chilli
salt
MANGO SALSA
1 mango, peeled and finely diced
½ small red onion, finely diced
1 fresh red chilli, cored, seeded and finely chopped
3 tablespoons chopped fresh coriander
grated rind and juice 1 lime

In a bowl, mix together hot pepper sauce, sugar, allspice, garlic, coriander and lime juice. Cut fish into cubes and add to the bowl. Stir to coat in the marinade, cover and leave in a cool place for 30 minutes. (See above.) Meanwhile, make the mango salsa. In a bowl, mix together mango, onion, chilli, coriander and lime rind and juice. Set aside. Remove the fish from the marinade, drain and arrange on a serving plate.

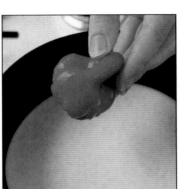

Heat the coconut milk and Scotch bonnet chilli in the fondue pot on top of the stove. Season with salt then transfer to the lighted spirit burner. Spear the fish on to the fondue forks and cook in the hot coconut milk for 2-3 minutes. Serve with the mango salsa.

Serves 4

PRAWNS IN JACKETS

2 sheets filo pastry approximately 45x25cm
  (18x10in)
25g (1oz/2 tablespoons) butter, melted
250g (9oz) (approximately 32) large raw prawns,
  peeled and thawed if frozen
salt and freshly ground black pepper
oil, for cooking
WASABI MAYONNAISE
150ml (5fl oz/⅔ cup) mayonnaise
1 teaspoon wasabi paste
2 teaspoons lime juice

Make the wasabi mayonnaise. In a bowl,
mix together mayonnaise, wasabi paste and
lime juice. Set aside.

Lightly brush sheets of filo pastry with
melted butter. Cut each sheet into strips
across. The strips should be as wide as the
prawns are long. Cut each strip in half
across. Dry prawns on paper towels and
season with salt and pepper. Roll a strip of
pastry round each prawn and arrange on a
serving dish.

Heat the oil in the fondue pot on top of the
stove then transfer to the lighted spirit
burner. Spear the wrapped prawns on the
fondue forks and cook in the hot oil for
2 minutes or until crisp and golden. Serve
with the wasabi mayonnaise.

Serves 4

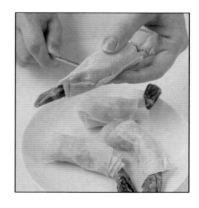

SEAFOOD FONDUE

225g (8oz) raw tiger prawns
550ml (20fl oz/2½ cups) good fish stock
½ lemon, sliced
1 small onion, peeled
225g (8oz) monkfish, skinned
225g (8oz) thick cod fillet, skinned
225g (8oz) scallops
lemon wedges and parsley sprigs, to garnish
Rouille (see page 86), to serve

Peel the prawns and place the shells in a saucepan with the stock, lemon and onion. Bring to the boil and simmer for 10 minutes.

Cut monkfish and cod into cubes and halve the scallops if they are large. Arrange on serving plates with the peeled prawns. Garnish with lemon wedges and parsley sprigs. Cover and keep cool.

Strain stock into the fondue pot, bring back to the boil on top of the stove then transfer to the lighted spirit burner. Spear the fish on to the fondue forks and cook in the hot stock for 2-3 minutes. Serve with Rouille.

Serves 6

VARIATION: The selection of fish can be varied according to personal preference and what is available.

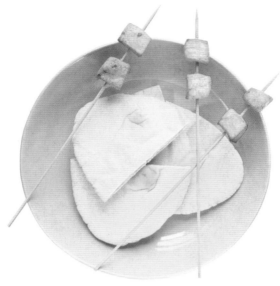

MARRAKESH SWORDFISH FONDUE

1 small red onion, finely chopped
2 cloves garlic, crushed
1 fresh red chilli, cored, seeded and finely chopped
2 tablespoons chopped fresh coriander
1 tablespoon chopped fresh mint
1 teaspoon ground cumin
1 teaspoon paprika
pinch saffron strands
4 tablespoons olive oil
juice 1 lemon
salt
700g (1½lb) swordfish, skinned
oil, for cooking
green salad and warm pitta bread, to serve

In a bowl, mix together the onion, garlic, chilli, coriander, mint, cumin, paprika, saffron, olive oil, lemon juice and season with salt. (See above.) Cut monkfish into cubes. Add them to spice mixture in the bowl. Mix well to coat, cover and leave in a cool place for 1 hour.

Using a slotted spoon, remove fish from the bowl and arrange on a serving plate. Heat oil in the fondue pot on top of the stove then transfer to the lighted spirit burner. Spear fish on to the fondue forks and cook in the hot oil for 2-3 minutes. Serve with salad and warm pitta bread.

Serves 4

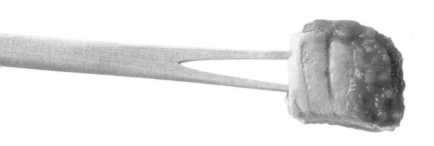

NIÇOISE FONDUE

1 tablespoon olive oil
1 onion, finely chopped
2 cloves garlic, crushed
400g (14oz) can chopped tomatoes
115ml (4fl oz/½ cup) dry white wine
1 teaspoon dried herbes de Provence
100g (3½oz) canned or bottled anchovies, drained
25g (1oz/2 tablespoons) pitted olives, chopped
salt and freshly ground black pepper
350g (12oz) cooked French beans, halved
3 hard boiled eggs, quartered
4 tablespoons vinaigrette dressing
450g (1lb) fresh tuna fish
French bread, to serve

Heat the oil in a pan, add onion and garlic and cook gently for 10 minutes or until soft. Add tomatoes, white wine, 70ml (2½fl oz/ ⅓ cup) water and herbes de Provence and simmer gently for about 10 minutes until well blended. (See above.) Process in a blender or food processor to make a smooth sauce then add anchovies and olives and process briefly until finely chopped. Season with salt and pepper and pour into the fondue pot.

Combine beans and eggs with vinaigrette dressing and place in a serving dish. Cut tuna fish into cubes and arrange on a serving dish. Heat tomato sauce on top of the stove until simmering then transfer to the lighted spirit burner. Spear cubes of tuna fish on fondue forks and cook in the hot tomato sauce for 2 minutes or until cooked as desired. Serve with the bean and egg salad and French bread.

Serves 4

PIRI PIRI PRAWNS

1 fresh red chilli, cored, seeded and very finely
  chopped
½ teaspoon paprika
½ teaspoon ground coriander
1 clove garlic, crushed
finely grated rind 1 lime
salt and freshly ground black pepper
250g (9oz) large raw prawns, peeled and thawed if
  frozen
oil, for cooking
lime wedges, to garnish
Aioli (see page 88) and bread, to serve

In a bowl, mix together chilli, paprika, ground
coriander, garlic, lime rind, salt and pepper.

Add prawns and mix well. Cover and leave
in a cool place for 30 minutes. Heat the oil
in the fondue pot on top of the stove then
transfer to the lighted spirit burner.

Thread prawns on to fondue forks or
bamboo skewers and cook in the hot oil for
1 minute or until pink. Serve, garnished
with lime wedges, with the aioli and bread.

Serves 4

BAGNA CAUDA

50g (2oz/¼ cup) butter
4 cloves garlic, crushed
50g (2oz) can anchovy fillets, drained and roughly
  chopped
150ml (5fl oz/⅔ cup) mild extra virgin olive oil
TO SERVE
a selection of raw and blanched vegetables such as
  celery, carrots, fennel, peppers, radishes, asparagus,
  cauliflower, baby artichoke hearts
hard boiled quails' eggs
breadsticks
toasted cubes of ciabatta bread

Arrange vegetables, eggs and bread on serving plates.

Gently heat butter in a heavy saucepan. Add garlic and cook gently, for 2 minutes. Add anchovies, then pour in oil very slowly, stirring constantly. Cook gently, stirring, for about 10 minutes. Do not allow to boil. The sauce in ready when anchovies have become a paste.

Transfer sauce to an earthenware bagna cauda pot or a fondue pot and place over the lighted spirit burner. To serve, dip vegetables, eggs and bread into the anchovy sauce.

Serves 4-6

CRISPY CRUMBED MUSSELS

1kg (2¼lb) fresh mussels in shells
2 lemons, quartered
6 cloves garlic, peeled
2 eggs, beaten
115g (4oz/2 cups) fresh breadcrumbs
oil, for cooking
lemon wedges, to garnish
Rouille (see page 86), to serve

Scrub mussels and remove the beards. Discard any which do not close when tapped sharply. Place mussels in a large pan with lemon quarters and garlic. Add 4 tablespoons of water to the pan.

Cover and cook on a high heat for a few minutes, shaking pan occasionally until mussels open. Discard any which remain closed. Drain mussels and remove from shells. Dry on paper towels. Place beaten egg and breadcrumbs in 2 separate shallow dishes. Dip the mussels into egg, allowing the excess to drip back, then dip in breadcrumbs. Place on a serving dish.

Heat the oil in the fondue pot on top of the stove then transfer to the lighted spirit burner. Thread the mussels, two at a time, on to fondue forks or bamboo skewers and cook in the hot oil for 1 minute or until crisp and golden. Serve, garnished with lemon wedges, with the rouille.

Serves 4

VARIATION: For a quick version of this dish, ready prepared breaded mussels, squid or scampi could be used.

THAI FISH CAKES

450g (1lb) boneless cod fillet
2 tablespoons chopped fresh coriander
1 tablespoon Thai red curry paste
1 small egg, beaten
1 teaspoon light muscovado sugar
1 tablespoon cornflour
1 teaspoon salt
oil, for cooking
lime wedges, to garnish
CHILLI DIPPING SAUCE
4 tablespoons rice vinegar
4 tablespoons soy sauce
1 teaspoon light muscovado sugar
1 clove garlic, crushed
1 fresh red chilli, cored, seeded and finely chopped
1 teaspoon sesame oil

Cut cod into chunks and chop roughly in a food processor. Add chopped coriander, curry paste, egg, sugar, cornflour and salt. Process again until well blended. Chill the mixture for 30 minutes. Divide mixture into 16 pieces, roll each into a ball then flatten slightly into a cake. Place on a serving dish and chill. (See above.) Make the dipping sauce. Place vinegar, soy sauce, sugar, garlic, chilli and sesame oil in a bowl and whisk together. Divide between small serving bowls.

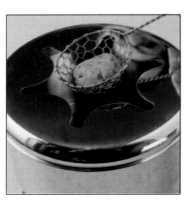

Heat oil in the fondue pot on top of the stove then transfer to the lighted spirit burner. To cook the fishcakes, place them in wire baskets and dip into hot oil for 2-3 minutes until golden and cooked through. Serve, garnished with lime wedges, with the dipping sauce.

Serves 4

FISH FIREPOT

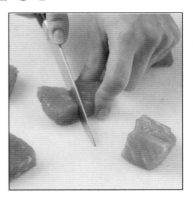

700g (1½lb) assorted boneless skinless fish such as
    salmon, cod and monkfish
225g (8oz) large raw peeled prawns or scallops or a
    mixture of both
450g (1lb) pak choi, cut into thin strips
225g (8oz) button mushrooms, halved
200g (7oz) fine egg noodles, cooked
chopped fresh coriander
1.75 litres (60fl oz/7½ cups) fish stock
3 tablespoons rice wine or dry sherry
1 teaspoon salt
DIPPING SAUCE
1 fresh red chilli, cored, seeded and finely chopped
2 cloves garlic, crushed
4 tablespoons soy sauce
1 tablespoon tamarind paste

Cut fish into thin slices and halve scallops if
they are large. (See above.) Arrange fish on
4 or 6 individual serving plates. Cover and
chill until required. Arrange pak choi,
mushrooms and noodles on serving plates.
Place chopped coriander in a shallow dish.
Make dipping sauce. In a bowl, mix together
chilli, garlic, soy sauce and tamarind paste.
If using a Mongolian hotpot, light it and
place on the table. Pour in stock and add
rice wine or sherry and salt. Bring to the boil.

(If using a fondue pot, pour stock and rice
wine or sherry into the pot, add salt and
bring to the boil on the stove. Transfer to the
lighted spirit burner.) Dip pieces of fish into
stock, using chopsticks or Chinese wire
strainers. Remove from stock and dip into
sauce or coriander before eating. From time
to time add mushrooms and pak choi to the
stock, and when cooked remove and eat.
Finally, add noodles to stock to heat through,
then serve the soup in warmed bowls.

Serves 6

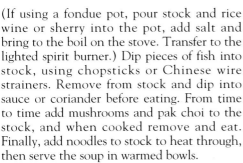

MANHATTAN FONDUE

8-10 bagels
115g (4oz) smoked salmon
400g (14oz/1¼ cups) cream cheese
175ml (6fl oz/¾ cup) milk
1 tablespoon chopped fresh dill
salt and freshly ground black pepper

Split the bagels, toast lightly and cut into bite sized pieces. Divide between 4-6 serving plates.

Chop smoked salmon into small pieces. Place cream cheese and milk in the fondue pot and heat gently on the stove until cheese has melted to a smooth sauce.

Stir in the dill and smoked salmon and season with salt and a generous amount of black pepper. Transfer the pot to the lighted spirit burner and keep warm over a low heat. Spear the pieces of bagel on fondue forks and dip into the sauce.

Serves 4-6

SMOKED FISH GOUJONS

4 heaped tablespoons plain flour
salt and freshly ground black pepper
700g (1½lb) skinless and boneless smoked fish fillets
3 eggs, beaten
115g (4oz/2 cups) fresh breadcrumbs
oil, for cooking
lemon wedges, to garnish
REMOULADE SAUCE
150ml (5fl oz/⅔ cup) mayonnaise
1 teaspoon Dijon mustard
2 teaspoons finely chopped capers
2 teaspoons finely chopped gherkins
2 teaspoons finely chopped fresh tarragon

To make the sauce mix together the mayonnaise, mustard, capers, gherkins and tarragon. Set aside. (See above.) Place flour in a shallow dish. Season with salt and pepper and mix together. Cut fish into strips about 1cm (½in) wide. Dust strips with seasoned flour. Place beaten egg and breadcrumbs in 2 separate shallow dishes. Dip each piece of fish in the egg allowing the excess to drip back in then dip in breadcrumbs. Place on a serving dish.

Heat oil in the fondue pot on top of the stove then transfer to the lighted spirit burner. Spear fish on to fondue forks and cook in oil for 1-2 minutes until crisp and golden. Serve, garnished with lemon wedges, with the sauce.

Serves 4

— ANCHOVY & PRAWN FONDUE —

50g (2oz) anchovy fillets, drained
1 clove garlic, halved
150ml (5fl oz/⅔ cup) dry white wine
115g (4oz/1 cup) grated Gruyère cheese
225g (8oz/2 cups) grated Cheddar cheese
1 teaspoon cornflour
2 tablespoons dry sherry
Tabasco sauce
TO SERVE
225g (8oz) large peeled cooked prawns
cubes of French bread

Place anchovy fillets in a mortar and pestle and pound to a paste. Arrange prawns and bread on serving plates.

Rub inside of a fondue pot with cut clove of garlic. Pour in wine and heat gently on the stove until bubbling. Gradually stir in cheeses. Heat gently, stirring, until the cheese has melted. In a small bowl, blend cornflour with the sherry.

Stir cornflour mixture into cheese and add Tabasco sauce, to taste, and anchovy paste. Cook gently, stirring until thick and creamy. Transfer pot to the lighted spirit burner. Serve with the prawns and bread.

Serves 4-6

— SWEET & SOUR FISH FONDUE —

2 eggs
115g (4oz/1 cup) plain flour
700g (1½lb) boneless skinless firm white fish
   such as monkfish, cut into cubes
oil, for cooking
SWEET & SOUR SAUCE
1 tablespoon oil
1 small onion, finely chopped
1 green pepper, seeded and sliced
1 teaspoon cornflour
2 tablespoons soft brown sugar
2 tablespoons white wine vinegar
2 tablespoons tomato purée
juice 1 small orange
2 tablespoons soy sauce
2 tablespoons finely chopped pineapple

To make sauce, heat oil in a saucepan. Add onion and cook for 5 minutes until beginning to soften. Add pepper and cook for 5 more minutes. In a small bowl, blend cornflour with 4 tablespoons water and add to the pan with sugar, vinegar, tomato purée, orange juice, soy sauce and pineapple. Bring to the boil, stirring, and cook until the sauce thickens. Keep warm.

Make the batter; whisk eggs with 200ml (7fl oz/scant 1 cup) iced water until frothy. Add flour and beat until just blended. Divide between 6 small bowls. Divide the fish between 6 serving plates. Heat oil in the fondue pot on top of the stove then transfer to the lighted spirit burner. Spear the fish on to the fondue forks, dip in the batter, then in hot oil for 2-3 minutes until batter is crisp and golden. Serve with the sweet and sour sauce.

Serves 6

FONDUE BOURGIGNONNE

1kg (2¼lb) lean fillet or rump steak
oil, for cooking
small baked potatoes and green salad, to serve
  (optional)
SAUCES
550ml (20fl oz/2½ cups) mayonnaise
50g (2oz) anchovies, drained
2 tablespoons horseradish sauce
2 tablespoons tomato purée
2 teaspoons hot pepper sauce
1 tablespoon curry paste

Cut steak into 2.5cm (1in) cubes and
arrange on 4-6 serving plates.

To make the sauces, divide mayonnaise
between 4 bowls. In a mortar and pestle,
pound anchovies to a purée and stir into
one of the bowls of mayonnaise. Stir
horseradish sauce into another, tomato
purée and hot pepper sauce into another
and curry paste into the last bowl. Transfer
sauces to small serving bowls.

Heat oil in the fondue pot on top of the
stove then transfer to the lighted spirit
burner. Spear steak on to fondue forks and
cook in hot oil according to individual taste.
Serve with the sauces, and baked potatoes
and salad, if you like.

Serves 6

VARIATIONS: Lean fillet of lamb could be
served instead of or as well as the steak.

CAJUN MEATBALLS

1 tablespoon oil
1 onion, finely chopped
1 teaspoon coriander seeds
½ teaspoon cardamom seeds
450g (1lb) lean minced steak
50g (2oz/1 cup) fresh breadcrumbs
1 small egg, beaten
grated rind ½ lemon
¼-½ teaspoon chilli powder
2 tablespoons chopped fresh coriander
salt and freshly ground black pepper
oil, for cooking
TO SERVE
Chilli Tomato Sauce (see page 87)
pitta bread
shredded lettuce

Heat oil in a saucepan. Add onion and cook for 10 minutes until soft. Set aside to cool. In a small heavy based saucepan, dry fry coriander and cardamom seeds for a few minutes until golden, then crush, using a mortar and pestle. In a bowl, mix together the onion, minced steak, crushed spices, breadcrumbs, egg, lemon rind, chilli powder, coriander, and salt and pepper until thoroughly combined.

Form the mixture into walnut sized balls. Arrange on serving plates and chill until required. Heat oil in the fondue pot on top of the stove then transfer to the lighted spirit burner. Spear meatballs on to the fondue forks and cook in the hot oil for 3-4 minutes until cooked. Serve with the sauce, pitta bread and lettuce.

Serves 4-6

KOFTAS & RAITA

1 small onion, roughly chopped
1 clove garlic, chopped
2.5cm (1in) piece fresh root ginger, peeled and chopped
1 teaspoon ground cumin
1 teaspoon ground coriander
1 tablespoon oil
450g (1lb) lean minced lamb
3 tablespoons chopped fresh coriander
salt and freshly ground black pepper
1 small egg, beaten
oil, for cooking
naan bread or chapatis, to serve
RAITA
½ cucumber
300ml (10fl oz/1½ cups) Greek yogurt
3 tablespoons chopped fresh mint

Put onion, garlic and ginger in a blender or food processor and chop finely, without turning to a paste. Add cumin and ground coriander and process briefly to blend. Heat oil in a frying pan, add onion mixture and cook for 2-3 minutes, stirring. (See above.) Leave to cool. In a bowl, mix together minced lamb, coriander, seasoning and cooled onion mixture. Mix thoroughly. Add just enough beaten egg to bind mixture together. With floured hands, roll mixture into bite sized balls. Arrange on serving plates and chill until required.

To make the raita, grate cucumber coarsely. Squeeze out as much liquid as possible then mix cucumber, yogurt and mint together. Season with salt and pepper and transfer to small serving bowls. Heat oil in the fondue pot on top of the stove then transfer to the lighted spirit burner. Spear the koftas on to fondue forks and cook in the hot oil for 3-4 minutes until cooked. Serve with the raita and naan bread or chapatis.

Serves 4-6

TURKISH LAMB

700g (1½lb) lean lamb
2 cloves garlic, crushed
4 tablespoons lemon juice
pinch chilli powder
1 teaspoon ground cumin
1 teaspoon ground coriander
½ teaspoon ground cinnamon
salt and freshly ground black pepper
oil, for cooking
TO SERVE
Tomato and Olive Salsa (see page 90)
pitta bread

Cut the lamb into 2.5cm (1in) cubes.

Crush garlic and place in a bowl. Add lemon juice, chilli powder, cumin, ground coriander and cinnamon, and stir. Add lamb and mix until well coated with marinade. Cover and leave to marinate in a cool place for 2 hours.

Remove lamb from marinade and pat dry with paper towels. Season with salt and pepper. Arrange the lamb on 4 serving plates. Heat the oil in the fondue pot on top of the stove then transfer to the lighted spirit burner. Spear the lamb on to fondue forks and cook in the hot oil for 3-4 minutes until cooked. Serve with the tomato and olive salsa.

Serves 4

PORK SATAY

1 teaspoon tamarind paste
2 cloves garlic, crushed
2 tablespoons soy sauce
1 teaspoon ground cumin
1 teaspoon ground coriander
½ teaspoon chilli powder
salt
450g (1lb) lean pork steaks
oil, for cooking
SATAY SAUCE
2 tablespoons smooth peanut butter
200ml (7fl oz/scant 1 cup) coconut cream
2 teaspoons red Thai curry paste
1 tablespoon fish sauce
1 tablespoon soft brown sugar

In a bowl mix together tamarind paste, garlic, soy sauce, ground cumin, ground coriander, chilli and salt. (See above.) Place pork steaks between 2 pieces of clear film and beat out flat with a meat hammer or rolling pin. Cut into strips then place in the bowl with marinade. Mix well then cover and leave in a cool place for 1 hour. Remove from marinade, dry with paper towels and thread on to bamboo skewers. Arrange on serving plates.

To make satay sauce, place peanut butter, coconut cream, red curry paste, fish sauce and brown sugar in a pan. Heat gently to form a smooth sauce, adding a little water if necessary. Keep warm. Heat oil in the fondue pot on top of the stove then transfer to the lighted spirit burner. Cook the skewers of pork in the hot oil for 3-4 minutes until cooked. Serve with the satay sauce.

Serves 4

– MEXICAN BEEF & GUACAMOLE –

700g (1½lb) sirloin or rump steak
2 teaspoons chilli sauce
2 cloves garlic, crushed
1 tablespoon chopped fresh coriander
1 teaspoon dried oregano
1 teaspoon ground cumin
juice 1 lime
tortilla chips, to serve
GUACAMOLE
2-3 ripe avocados, depending on the size
½ red onion, finely chopped
1 tablespoon chopped fresh coriander
1 clove garlic, crushed
1 red chilli, cored, seeded and finely chopped
2 tomatoes, peeled, seeded and finely chopped
juice ½ -1 lime
pinch sugar
salt and freshly ground black pepper

Cut steak into 2.5cm (1in) cubes. In a bowl, mix together chilli sauce, garlic, coriander, oregano, cumin and lime juice. Add steak and mix well. (See above.) Cover and set aside in the fridge for 1-2 hours. Meanwhile, make guacamole. Peel and stone avocados, place in a bowl and mash with a fork. Do not make mixture too smooth. Stir in onion, coriander, garlic, chilli and tomato. Then stir in lime juice, sugar, salt and pepper to taste.

Leave to stand for 30 minutes, but no longer than 1 hour. Just before serving, stir again and transfer to small serving bowls. Remove steak from marinade, dry with paper towels and arrange on serving plates. Heat oil in the fondue pot on top of the stove then transfer to the lighted spirit burner. Spear cubes of steak on to fondue forks and cook in hot oil for 3-4 minutes until cooked. Serve with guacamole and tortilla chips.

Serves 4-6

TERIYAKI STEAK

700g (1½lb) fillet steak
5cm (2in) piece fresh root ginger
1 tablespoon oil
1 clove garlic, crushed
4 tablespoons soy sauce
2 tablespoons mirin or medium sherry
1 teaspoon soft light brown sugar
freshly ground black pepper
TO SERVE
1 daikon radish
2 tablespoons wasabi paste
coriander sprigs

Cut the steaks into thin strips 1cm (½in) wide and 10cm (4in) long.

Peel ginger and grate into a bowl. Squeeze out liquid and put 1 tablespoon in a dish with oil, garlic, soy sauce, mirin or sherry and sugar. Add steak, mix well, cover and leave to marinate in the fridge for 1 hour. Meanwhile, prepare garnish. Peel daikon radish and grate into a bowl. Squeeze out as much liquid as possible and divide the grated radish between 4 serving plates. Place a little wasabi paste and a sprig of coriander on each plate.

Remove steak from marinade and pat dry with paper towels. Season with pepper. Thread strips of steak on to bamboo skewers and divide between 4 serving dishes. Heat oil in the fondue pot on top of the stove then transfer to the lighted spirit burner. Cook the steak in hot oil for 2-3 minutes until cooked. Serve with daikon radish and wasabi, garnished with coriander.

Serves 4

— CURRIED APRICOT TURKEY —

1 tablespoon oil
1 onion, finely chopped
1 clove garlic, crushed
2 bay leaves
juice 1 lemon
2 tablespoons curry powder
4 tablespoons apricot jam
4 tablespoons apple juice
salt
700g (1½lb) turkey fillet
4 tablespoons crème fraîche
oil, for cooking

Heat oil in a saucepan. Add onion, garlic and bay leaves and cook for 10 minutes until soft.

Add lemon juice, curry powder, apricot jam, apple juice and salt, to taste. Cook gently for 5 minutes. Transfer to a bowl and leave to cool. Cut turkey into 2.5cm (1in) cubes and add to cooled marinade. Mix well, cover and leave to marinate in the fridge for 2 hours.

Remove turkey and allow marinade to run back into the bowl. Dry turkey with paper towels and arrange on 4 serving plates. Transfer marinade to a pan and simmer for 2 minutes. Stir in crème fraîche. Heat oil in the fondue pot on top of the stove then transfer to the lighted spirit burner. Spear turkey on to fondue forks and cook in hot oil for 3-4 minutes until cooked. Serve with the sauce.

Serves 4

PROVENÇAL BEEF

2 cloves garlic, crushed
150ml (5fl oz/⅔ cup) red wine
grated rind and juice ½ orange
1 tablespoon chopped fresh rosemary
1 teaspoon dried herbes de provence
2 tablespoons olive oil
55g (1¼lb) rump or fillet steak
salt and freshly ground black pepper
oil, for cooking
TOMATO SALAD
450g (1lb) tomatoes, sliced
6 spring onions, thinly sliced
2 tablespoons shredded basil leaves
1 clove garlic, crushed
6 tablespoons olive oil
2 tablespoons balsamic vinegar

In a bowl, mix together garlic, wine, orange
rind and juice, rosemary, herbes de provence
and olive oil. Cut beef into 2.5cm (1in)
cubes and add to marinade. Cover and
marinate overnight in the refrigerator.
Meanwhile, make salad. Arrange sliced
tomatoes on individual serving plates.
Sprinkle spring onions and basil over
tomatoes. In a small bowl, whisk together
garlic, olive oil, balsamic vinegar, salt and
pepper. Pour over tomatoes, cover and leave
to marinate for 1 hour.

Remove beef from marinade and dry on
paper towels. Season with salt and pepper
and arrange on serving plates. Heat oil in
the fondue pot on top of the stove then
transfer to the lighted spirit burner. Spear
the beef on to fondue forks and cook in hot
oil for 3-4 minutes until cooked. Serve with
the tomato salad.

Serves 4

JERK CHICKEN

grated rind and juice 1 lime
2.5cm (1in) piece fresh root ginger
3 tablespoons olive oil
1 clove garlic, crushed
1 teaspoon dried thyme
1 teaspoon ground cinnamon
1 teaspoon ground allspice
1 teaspoon soft brown sugar
2 teaspoons hot pepper sauce
salt and freshly ground black pepper
900g (2lb) skinless, boneless chicken breast
lime wedges, to garnish
oil, for frying
Bean Salad (see page 92), to serve

Grate rind from lime and squeeze juice into a bowl. Peel ginger and grate into the bowl. Add olive oil, garlic, thyme, cinnamon, allspice, sugar, hot pepper sauce, salt and pepper. Mix together. (See above.) Cut chicken into 2.5cm (1in) cubes and add to marinade. Cover and leave in a cool place to marinate for 2 hours.

Remove chicken from marinade, pat dry with paper towels and arrange on serving plates. Garnish with lime wedges. Heat oil in the fondue pot on top of the stove then transfer to the lighted spirit burner. Spear chicken on to fondue forks and cook in hot oil for 3-4 minutes until cooked. Serve with the salad.

Serves 6

CHICKEN TIKKA

5cm (2in) piece fresh root ginger
4 tablespoons natural yogurt
1-2 tablespoons hot Madras curry paste
2 cloves garlic, crushed
1 teaspoon turmeric
2 tablespoons lemon juice
1 teaspoon paprika
½ teaspoon salt
700g (1½lb) skinless, boneless chicken breasts
coriander sprigs and lemon wedges, to garnish
oil, for cooking
TO SERVE
Raita (see page 28)
naan bread
poppadoms

Peel ginger and grate into a bowl. Add the yogurt, curry paste, garlic, turmeric, lemon juice, paprika and salt. Mix together thoroughly. (See above.) Cut chicken into 2cm (¾in) cubes. Add to marinade and mix well. Cover and leave in the fridge to marinate for at least 2 hours. Remove from marinade and allow as much of the marinade to drain off as possible.

Thread chicken cubes, 2 or 3 together, on to bamboo skewers and arrange on serving plates, garnished with coriander and lemon wedges. Heat oil in the fondue pot on top of the stove then transfer to the lighted spirit burner. Cook chicken in hot oil for 3-4 minutes until cooked. Serve with the raita, naan bread and poppadoms.

Serves 4

FIVE SPICE DUCK

3-4 duck breasts, about 700g (1½lb) total weight
1 teaspoon sesame oil
3 tablespoons soy sauce
3 tablespoons rice wine or dry sherry
1 tablespoon honey
1 tablespoon lime juice
2 teaspoons five spice powder
1 clove garlic, crushed
2.5cm (1in) piece fresh root ginger, grated
lime wedges, to garnish
oil, for cooking
TO SERVE
shredded spring onions
shredded celery
hoisin or plum sauce
Chinese pancakes or flour tortillas

Remove skin and fat from duck breasts and cut meat into thin strips. Place in a shallow dish. In a bowl, mix together sesame oil, soy sauce, rice wine or sherry, honey, lime juice, five spice powder, garlic and ginger. (See above.) Pour over duck and stir well. Cover and leave in a cool place to marinate for 30 minutes. Remove duck strips from marinade and dry on paper towels. Arrange on serving plates and garnish with lime wedges. Arrange spring onions and celery on serving plates and place hoisin or plum sauce in small bowls.

Warm Chinese pancakes or tortillas and keep warm. Heat oil in the fondue pot on top of the stove then transfer to the lighted spirit burner. Spear strips of duck on to fondue forks, or thread on to bamboo skewers. Cook in hot oil for 3-4 minutes until cooked. To serve, spread a little hoisin or plum sauce on a pancake or tortilla, add some spring onion and celery and place a few strips of cooked duck on top then roll up.

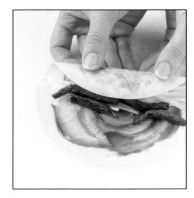

Serves 4-6

TURKEY NUGGETS

700g (1½lb) turkey fillets
3 tablespoons plain flour
salt and freshly ground black pepper
115g (4oz/1 cup) dry breadcrumbs
2 teaspoons finely grated lemon rind
2 large eggs, beaten
lemon wedges, to garnish
oil, for frying
HERB DIP
200gm (7oz) fromage frais
1 clove garlic, crushed
2 tablespoons chopped fresh tarragon
1 tablespoon chopped fresh chives
1 tablespoon chopped fresh chervil
salt and freshly ground black pepper

Cut turkey into bite sized cubes. In a bowl, mix together flour, salt and pepper. In a shallow dish, mix together breadcrumbs and lemon rind. Pour beaten egg into another shallow dish. Toss turkey cubes in seasoned flour, dip in beaten egg then coat in breadcrumbs. (See above.) Arrange on serving plates and garnish with lemon wedges. To make herb dip, place fromage frais in a bowl, add garlic, tarragon, chives and chervil and season with salt and pepper. Mix well together then divide between small serving bowls.

Heat oil in the fondue pot on top of the stove then transfer to the lighted spirit burner. Spear turkey nuggets on to fondue forks and cook in hot oil for 3-4 minutes until cooked. Serve with the herb dip.

Serves 4-6

VARIATION: Chicken may be used as an alternative to turkey.

— HARISSA SPICED CHICKEN —

2 teaspoons coriander seeds
1½ teaspoons cumin seeds
2 cloves garlic
1-2 tablespoons chilli paste
½ teaspoon salt
4 tablespoons olive oil
700g (1½lb) skinless, boneless chicken breasts
oil, for cooking
Couscous Salad (see page 93), to serve
TOMATO & PRESERVED LEMON SALSA
3-4 ripe tomatoes
½ preserved lemon
2 spring onions, chopped
2 tablespoons liquid from the preserved lemons
1 tablespoon chopped fresh mint
salt and freshly ground black pepper

Heat a heavy based frying pan. Add coriander and cumin seeds, and dry fry, stirring, for 2 or 3 minutes until they give off a fragrant aroma. (See above.) Grind to a powder in a mortar and pestle. Place ground seeds in a bowl with garlic, chilli paste, salt and olive oil. Mix together. Cut chicken into cubes and add to marinade. Cover and leave in the fridge for 1 hour. Make the salsa. Cut tomatoes into dice and place in a bowl. Remove flesh from preserved lemon and cut skin into dice.

Add to tomatoes with spring onion, preserved lemon liquid, mint, salt and pepper. Transfer to small serving bowls. Remove chicken from marinade and dry with paper towels. Arrange on serving plates. Heat oil in the fondue pot on top of the stove then transfer to the lighted spirit burner. Spear chicken on to fondue forks and cook in hot oil for 3-4 minutes. Serve with the salsa and couscous.

Serves 4

—— THAI CHICKEN MEATBALLS ——

450g (1lb) minced chicken
4 spring onions, chopped
2 tablespoons chopped fresh coriander
2 tablespoons Thai green curry paste
1 teaspoon light muscovado sugar
1 teaspoon salt
lime wedges, to garnish
oil, for cooking
DIPPING SAUCE
1 fresh red chilli, cored, seeded and finely chopped
2 tablespoons light soy sauce
1 tablespoons Thai fish sauce
1 tablespoon lime juice
2 tablespoons soft brown sugar

In a bowl, mix together chicken, spring onions, coriander, curry paste, sugar and salt. (See above.) Form into small balls. Cover and chill for 30 minutes. Make the dipping sauce. Place chilli, soy sauce, fish sauce, lime juice and sugar in a bowl and mix together. Divide between 4 small dip dishes.

Arrange chicken balls on serving plates and garnish with lime wedges. Heat oil in the fondue pot on top of the stove then transfer to the lighted spirit burner. Spear chicken balls on to fondue forks and cook in hot oil for 3-4 minutes. Serve with the dipping sauce.

Serves 4

THAI CHICKEN HOTPOT

900g (2lb) boneless chicken breast
12 button mushrooms
12 spring onions, cut into 5cm (2in) lengths
1 red pepper, seeded and cut into strips
115g (4oz) baby sweetcorn
115g (4oz) mange-tout
1 bunch watercress
115g (4oz) fine egg noodles, broken into pieces
850ml (30fl oz/3¼ cups) good chicken stock
2 small red chillies
3 kaffir lime leaves
1 stalk lemon grass, crushed
2 slices fresh galangal or ginger
1 carrot, cut into thin matchsticks
6 Chinese leaves, shredded
dipping sauce (see page 40), to serve

Cut chicken into thin strips, place on 6 serving plates, cover and chill until required. Divide mushrooms, spring onions, pepper, sweetcorn, mange-tout and watercress between 6 plates, cover and chill until required. Soak the egg noodles in boiling water for 3-4 minutes, then drain and transfer to a serving bowl. (See above.) Place stock in a saucepan or fondue pot. Add chillies, lime leaves, lemon grass and galangal or ginger. Bring to the boil and simmer gently for 10 minutes. Add carrot.

Either transfer stock to a hot pot or transfer the fondue pot to the spirit burner. Using chopsticks or Chinese wire strainers, cook chicken and vegetables in the stock then dip in the dipping sauce to eat. When this is completed, add noodles and Chinese leaves and ladle noodle soup into warmed bowls.

Serves 6-8

PUMPKIN FONDUE

4 small pumpkins or squash, the size of a grapefruit
300g (10oz) creamy blue cheese such as Dolcelatte
225ml (8fl oz/1 cup) double cream
4 tablespoons fresh white breadcrumbs
2 teaspoons chopped fresh sage
salt and freshly ground black pepper
HERB BREADSTICKS:
500g (1lb) packet ciabatta bread mix
1 tablespoon dried oregano
1 tablespoon caraway seeds
oil, for brushing
flour, for dusting

Preheat the oven to 230C (450F/Gas 8). To make breadsticks, follow packet instructions to after first rising of dough.

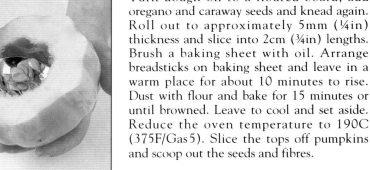

Turn dough on to a floured board, add oregano and caraway seeds and knead again. Roll out to approximately 5mm (¼in) thickness and slice into 2cm (¾in) lengths. Brush a baking sheet with oil. Arrange breadsticks on baking sheet and leave in a warm place for about 10 minutes to rise. Dust with flour and bake for 15 minutes or until browned. Leave to cool and set aside. Reduce the oven temperature to 190C (375F/Gas 5). Slice the tops off pumpkins and scoop out the seeds and fibres.

Crumble half the cheese into pumpkins; top with half the cream. Scatter 1 tablespoon of breadcrumbs in each pumpkin then top with remaining cheese and cream. Scatter sage over and season with salt and pepper. Replace tops on pumpkins then place in an ovenproof dish. Bake for 45 minutes or until cheese is bubbling and pumpkins are soft. Serve with breadsticks to dip in then scrape out pumpkin flesh with a spoon.

Serves 4

— CHEESE & TOMATO FONDUE —

500g (1lb) carton passata
200g (7oz/scant 1 cup) cream cheese
sugar, to taste
few drops Tabasco sauce
salt and freshly ground black pepper
frankfurters and cubes of ham, to serve
CORNMEAL MUFFINS:
50g (2oz/½ cup) self-raising flour
1½ teaspoons baking powder
salt and freshly ground black pepper
115g (4oz/1 cup) fine cornmeal
50g (2 oz/½ cup) grated Cheddar cheese
25g (1 oz/2 tablespoons) butter, melted
1 large egg, beaten
150ml (5fl oz/⅔ cup) milk

Preheat the oven to 200C (400F/Gas6).
Line 12 mini muffin pans with paper mini
muffin cases. To make the muffins, sift flour,
baking powder, salt and pepper into a bowl
then stir in cornmeal and cheese. (See
above.) In a bowl, mix together butter, egg
and milk. Pour on to the dry ingredients and
mix quickly until just combined. Do not
overmix. Spoon the batter into prepared
muffin cases. Bake for 10-15 minutes until
well risen and golden brown. Leave to cool.
Arrange on serving plates with the
frankfurters and ham.

Place passata and cream cheese in a fondue
pot and heat gently until cheese has melted.
Add sugar, Tabasco sauce, salt and pepper
to taste. Heat until just below simmering
point then transfer to the fondue burner.
Serve with the corn muffins, frankfurters
and ham for dipping.

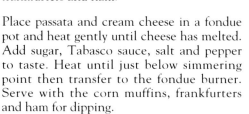

Serves 4-6

TEMPURA

oil, for frying
450g (1lb) assorted vegetables, such as red pepper
    strips, aubergine and courgette batons, spring onions,
    mushrooms, mange-tout, baby sweetcorn, asparagus
BATTER:
115g (4oz/1 cup) plain flour
1 egg, separated
1 teaspoon olive oil
salt and freshly ground black pepper
DIPPING SAUCE:
2 teaspoons each sesame oil, red wine vinegar and soy
    sauce
3 tablespoons ginger syrup (from jar of ginger)
2 tablespoons clear honey
4 spring onions, finely sliced

To make the batter, sift flour into a bowl.
Measure 225ml (8fl oz/1 cup) iced water
into a jug and whisk in egg yolk and olive
oil. Season with salt and pepper. Make a
well in the middle of flour and gradually
whisk in liquid. (See above.) Cover and
stand for 1 hour. To make the dipping
sauce, mix together the sesame oil, red wine
vinegar, soy sauce, ginger syrup and honey.
Transfer to small dishes and sprinkle the
spring onions on top.

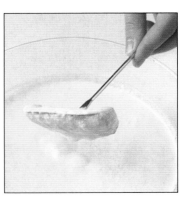

Whisk egg white until stiff then fold into
the batter. Heat oil in the fondue pot on top
of the stove then transfer to the lighted
spirit burner. To serve, dip vegetables into
batter then into hot oil for 1-2 minutes until
crisp and browned. Alternatively, spear two
or three pieces of vegetables on to skewers
and cook in the hot oil. Serve with the
dipping sauce.

Serves 4

FALAFEL FONDUE

225g (8oz/1 cup) dried chickpeas, soaked overnight
  in cold water and drained
2 tablespoons chopped fresh parsley
1 tablespoon chopped fresh coriander
1 tablespoon tahini paste
1 clove garlic, crushed
1 tablespoon lemon juice
salt and freshly ground black pepper
seasoned flour, for dusting
oil, for frying
warm pitta bread, to serve
CHILLI YOGURT DIP:
150ml (5fl oz/⅔ cup) Greek style yogurt
1 fresh red chilli, cored, seeded and finely chopped
2 tablespoons chopped fresh coriander

Process chickpeas in a blender or food
processor until as smooth as possible.
Transfer to a bowl and stir in parsley,
coriander, tahini, garlic, lemon juice and
salt and pepper. (See above.) Cover and set
aside for 30 minutes. To make the chilli dip,
in a bowl, mix together the yogurt, chilli,
coriander, salt and pepper. Transfer to a
serving bowl and set aside.

With floured hands, roll the chickpea
mixture into 2.5cm (1in) balls. Dust with
seasoned flour. Arrange on serving plates.
Heat oil in the fondue pot on top of the
stove then transfer to the lighted spirit
burner. Spear the falafel on to fondue forks
and cook in the hot oil for 2 minutes or
until evenly browned. Serve with the chilli
yogurt dip and warm pitta bread.

Serves 4

ONION BHAJI FONDUE

4 tablespoons gram flour
½ teaspoon turmeric
½ teaspoon ground cumin
½ teaspoon ground coriander
1 teaspoon garam masala
pinch cayenne pepper
1 egg, beaten
1 large onion, quartered and very thinly sliced
1 tablespoon chopped fresh coriander
oil, for frying
MINTED YOGURT DIP:
225ml (8fl oz/1 cup) Greek style natural yogurt
1 clove garlic, crushed
3 tablespoons chopped fresh mint
salt and freshly ground black pepper

To make the dip, in a bowl mix together yogurt, garlic, mint, salt and pepper. (See above.) Transfer to serving bowls and set aside. Put the gram flour, turmeric, cumin, coriander, garam masala and cayenne pepper in a bowl and mix together. Stir in egg, season with salt and pepper then add sliced onion and chopped coriander. Heat the oil in the fondue pot on top of the stove then transfer to the lighted spirit burner.

To cook the bhajis, push teaspoons of mixture into oil with another spoon. Cook a few at a time for 2-3 minutes until crisp and golden. Remove from oil with Chinese wire nets. Serve with the yogurt dip.

Serves 4 as an appetiser

SPRING ROLLS

1 tablespoon oil
1 teaspoon sesame oil
1 clove garlic, crushed
1 fresh red chilli, cored, seeded and finely sliced
450g (1lb) pack fresh stir-fry vegetables
2cm (½in) piece fresh root ginger, grated
1 tablespoon dry sherry or rice wine
1 tablespoon soy sauce
salt and freshly ground black pepper
12 spring roll wrappers
1 small egg, beaten
lime wedges and fresh coriander, to garnish
oil, for frying
Dipping Sauce (see page 44), to serve

Heat oils in a wok. Add garlic and chilli.

Stir-fry for 30 seconds. Add vegetables and ginger and stir-fry for 1 minute more, then drizzle sherry or rice wine and soy sauce over. Allow mixture to bubble up for 1 minute. Season with salt and pepper. Using a slotted spoon, transfer the vegetables to a dish. Set aside until cool. Soften the spring roll wrappers, following the directions on the packet. Place a spoonful of filling on a wrapper.

Fold over front edge and sides and roll up neatly, sealing edges with a little beaten egg. Repeat with remaining wrappers and filling. Divide spring rolls between 4 serving plates. Garnish with lime wedges and coriander. Heat oil in the fondue pot on top of the stove then transfer to the lighted spirit burner. Dip rolls into oil, using fondue forks or Chinese wire baskets. Cook for 2 minutes or until crisp. Serve with the dipping sauce.

Serves 4

— WILD MUSHROOM FONDUE —

7g (¼oz) dried wild mushrooms
3 tablespoons olive oil
4 shallots, finely chopped
2 cloves garlic, crushed
115g (4oz) fresh mixed wild mushrooms, chopped
3 tablespoons plain flour
225ml (8fl oz/1 cup) dry cider
350g (12oz) Emmental cheese, grated
115g (4oz) Roquefort cheese, crumbled
1 tablespoon chopped fresh tarragon
2 tablespoons single cream
TO SERVE:
cubes of ham, cherry tomatoes, cooked asparagus
  spears and cubes of bread

Place dried mushrooms in a bowl and cover with boiling water. Leave to soak for 20 minutes. Drain, reserving 115ml (4fl oz/ ½ cup) of soaking liquid. Chop soaked mushrooms finely. (See above.) In the fondue pot, heat the oil. Add shallots and garlic and cook for 5 minutes until soft. Add dried and fresh mushrooms and cook for a further 4-5 minutes until soft. Stir in flour and cook for 2 minutes. Gradually stir in reserved soaking liquid, then add cider.

Cook gently, stirring, until the mixture thickens then gradually stir in Emmental and Roquefort cheeses. Add the tarragon and continue to cook gently, stirring until the cheese is melted and the mixture is smooth and creamy. Stir in cream. Transfer pot to the lighted burner and serve with the ham, vegetables and bread to dip in.

Serves 6

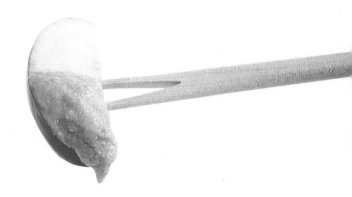

AVOCADO FONDUE

2 avocados
1 tablespoon lime juice
1 clove garlic
225ml (8fl oz/1 cup) dry white wine
350g (12oz) Gruyère cheese, grated
1 tablespoon cornflour
salt and freshly ground black pepper
4 tablespoons sour cream
TO SERVE:
pickled jalapeño chillies, slices of apple, breadsticks,
　large peeled prawns

Halve avocados and remove stone. Using a
teaspoon, scoop out flesh and place in a bowl.
Scrape out all bright green flesh next to skin.

Mash avocado until smooth then stir in
lime juice. Cut garlic in half and rub round
inside of the fondue pot. Pour in wine and
heat until bubbling. In a bowl, toss together
cheese and cornflour then stir into the wine.
Cook gently, stirring, until cheese has
melted.

Add avocado and cook, stirring, until
smooth and heated through. Season with
salt and pepper then stir in sour cream.
Transfer the pot to the lighted burner and
serve with the chillies, apple, breadsticks
and prawns for dipping.

Serves 4-6

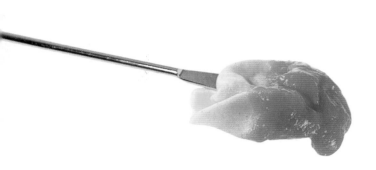

— PEPPER & TOMATO FONDUE —

6 large tomatoes
4 red peppers
5 tablespoons olive oil
1 clove garlic, chopped
salt and freshly ground black pepper
1 onion, finely chopped
150ml (5fl oz/⅔ cup) vegetable or chicken stock
2 tablespoons cornflour, blended with a little water
fresh ravioli, cooked, to serve

Preheat the oven to 190C (350F/Gas 5). Oil 2 roasting tins. Cut tomatoes in half and cut red peppers into quarters and remove the seeds.

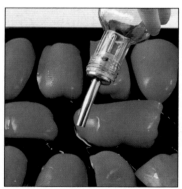

Place tomatoes, cut side up, in one of the roasting tins. Drizzle with 2 tablespoons of the olive oil and scatter with garlic. Season with salt and pepper. Place peppers in the other tin and drizzle with 2 tablespoons olive oil. Put tomatoes and peppers in the oven and roast tomatoes for 45-60 minutes until beginning to blacken round the edges. Cook the peppers, turning occasionally, until their skins are charred and blistered. Put in a plastic bag, seal and leave until cool enough to handle, then peel and chop coarsely.

Heat remaining oil in a pan. Cook onion, stirring occasionally, for 5-10 minutes, until soft. Add peppers and stock. Cover and simmer for 15 minutes. Transfer to a blender or food processor, add tomatoes and process until smooth. Press through a sieve and pour into the fondue pot. Heat on the stove until almost simmering. Stir cornflour into mixture. Simmer for a few minutes until thickened then transfer to the lighted fondue burner. Serve with the ravioli.

Serves 4

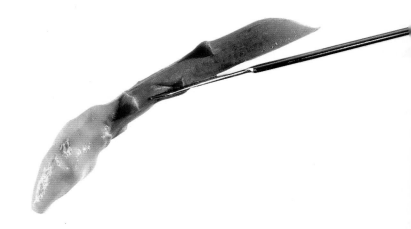

ASPARAGUS FONDUE

425g (15oz) canned asparagus spears
1 clove garlic, halved
225ml (8fl oz/1 cup) dry white wine
350g (12oz) Edam cheese, grated
1 tablespoon cornflour
4 tablespoons crème fraîche
salt and freshly ground black pepper
TO SERVE:
blanched fresh asparagus spears, cooked baby
  artichoke hearts, cubes of French bread

Drain asparagus and process in a blender or food processor until smooth. Set aside.

Rub the inside of the fondue pot with garlic, then pour in wine and heat until bubbling. Gradually stir in cheese and cook, stirring, over a low heat, until cheese has melted. Blend together cornflour and crème fraîche and stir into cheese mixture. Continue to cook for a few more minutes until thick and smooth.

Stir in asparagus purée and season with salt and pepper. Cook for another minute until heated through. Transfer the pot to the lighted burner. Serve with the asparagus spears, artichoke hearts and bread.

Serves 4-6

— CAULIFLOWER CHEESE —

1 cauliflower
crisp fried onions, to garnish
CHEESE SAUCE:
15g (½oz/1 tablespoon) butter
2 shallots, finely chopped
15g (½oz/2 tablespoons) plain flour
300ml (10fl oz/1½ cups) milk
50g (2 oz/½ cup) grated Cheddar cheese
25g (1oz/¼ cup) grated Parmesan cheese
1 teaspoon Dijon mustard
pinch cayenne pepper
salt

Cut cauliflower into florets. Bring a pan of salted water to the boil.

Add cauliflower and boil for 5 minutes or until just tender. Drain thoroughly and divide between 4 serving plates. To make the cheese sauce, place butter in a saucepan and heat gently until melted. Add shallots and cook for 5 minutes until soft. Stir in flour and cook for 1 minute. Remove the pan from the heat and gradually stir in milk. Return the pan to the heat and bring to the boil then simmer gently, stirring for 2 minutes.

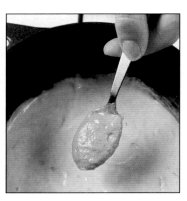

Stir in Cheddar cheese, Parmesan cheese, mustard and cayenne pepper. Season with salt. Transfer the fondue pot to the lighted spirit burner. Scatter fried onions over the top. Spear the cauliflower florets on to fondue forks and dip into the sauce.

Serves 4

— THAI SWEETCORN FONDUE —

400g (14oz) canned sweetcorn
300ml (10fl oz/1¼ cups) chicken stock
200ml (7fl oz/scant 1 cup) coconut cream
1 tablespoon Thai green curry paste
1 tablespoon Thai fish sauce
2 tablespoons cornflour
2 tablespoons chopped fresh coriander
TO SERVE:
blanched baby sweetcorn and mange-tout
mini poppadoms
cooked peeled prawns

Drain sweetcorn. In a blender or food processor, process sweetcorn to a purée and transfer to the fondue pot.

Stir in stock, coconut cream, Thai green curry paste and fish sauce. Place over a medium heat and bring to the boil, stirring. Blend cornflour with 2 tablespoons of cold water and add to the mixture. Bring to the boil and cook, stirring for 1 minute or until the mixture thickens.

Stir in the chopped coriander. Transfer the pot to the lighted fondue burner and serve with the baby sweetcorn, mange-tout, poppadoms and prawns.

Serves 4

NOTE: Vary the amount of Thai green curry sauce according to taste. For children, add a little less and for those who prefer a more fiery flavour, add more.

FONDUE SAVOYARDE

1 clove garlic, cut in half
150ml (5fl oz/²⁄₃ cup) dry white wine
1 teaspoon lemon juice
225g (8oz/2 cups) grated Gruyère cheese
225g (8oz/2 cups) grated Emmental cheese
1 tablespoon cornflour
2 tablespoons kirsch
pinch freshly grated nutmeg
pinch cayenne pepper
TO SERVE
cubes of baguette
green salad
slices of air dried ham

Rub cut side of garlic round inside fondue pot.

Pour wine and lemon juice into the pot and place over a low heat. Heat gently until bubbling. Gradually stir in grated cheeses and heat gently, stirring, until completely melted. In a small bowl, blend together the cornflour and kirsch and stir into cheese mixture.

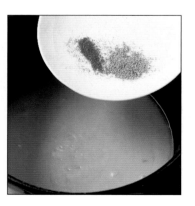

Continue to cook, stirring, for 2-3 minutes until mixture is thick and creamy. Add nutmeg and cayenne pepper. Transfer pot to the lighted spirit burner. To serve, spear cubes of bread on to the fondue forks and dip into cheese mixture. Serve with the salad and air dried ham.

Serves 4-6

GOUDA CHEESE FONDUE

½ small onion
2 teaspoons cumin seeds
150ml (5fl oz/⅔ cup) dry white wine
1 teaspoon lemon juice
400g (14oz/3½ cups) grated Gouda cheese
2 teaspoons cornflour
2 tablespoons gin
freshly ground black pepper
pinch nutmeg
light rye bread cubes, to serve

Rub inside of the fondue pot with cut side of onion. Place cumin seeds in pot and heat gently for 1 minute.

Add wine and lemon juice. Heat until nearly boiling and then add grated cheese. Heat gently, stirring, until cheese melts. In a small bowl blend together cornflour and gin. Stir into cheese mixture.

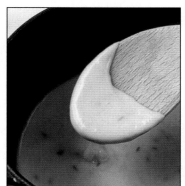

As soon as fondue thickens and comes just to a simmer, take off the heat. Season with pepper and nutmeg. Place the fondue pot over the lighted spirit burner and serve with the rye bread.

Serves 4

FONDUE INDIENNE

1 clove garlic, halved
350g (12oz/3 cups) grated Cheddar cheese
2 tablespoons plain flour
1 small onion, grated
300ml (10fl oz/1½ cups) dry white wine
2 teaspoons curry paste
2 tablespoons mango chutney
salt and freshly ground black pepper
cayenne pepper, to garnish
naan bread, to serve

Rub the inside of the fondue pot with the cut clove of garlic. Crush the garlic.

Place cheese and flour in a plastic bag and toss to combine. Place crushed garlic, onion, wine and curry paste in the fondue pot and bring almost to a simmer. Gradually stir in cheese, allowing it to melt between each addition.

Stir in mango chutney and salt and pepper to taste. Place on the lighted spirit burner. Sprinkle a little cayenne pepper over. Serve with pieces of naan bread.

Serves 4

NOTE: If the mango chutney has large pieces of fruit in it, chop it finely.

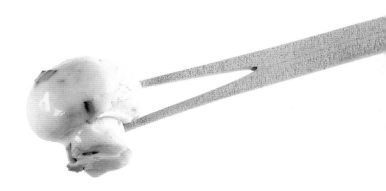

FRENCH BRIE FONDUE

375g (13oz) ripe French Brie
50g (2oz/¼ cup) butter
1 onion, finely chopped
1 clove garlic, crushed
25g (1oz/¼ cup) plain flour
300ml (10fl oz/1¼ cups) chicken or vegetable stock
150ml (5fl oz/⅔ cup) double cream
1 tablespoon chopped fresh tarragon
salt and freshly ground black pepper
TO SERVE
grapes
cubes of French bread
raw button mushrooms

Cut away rind from Brie and slice cheese thinly. Set aside.

Melt butter in the fondue pot over a low heat. Add onion and garlic and cook gently for 10 minutes until softened. Sprinkle flour over and cook for 1-2 minutes, stirring. Gradually add stock and continue to stir until mixture thickens. Simmer gently for 2-3 minutes.

Stir sliced Brie and cream into the fondue. Cook, stirring, until cheese has melted and mixture is smooth. Stir in tarragon and season with salt and pepper. Transfer the fondue pot to the lighted spirit burner. To serve, spear grapes, bread and mushrooms on to skewers or fondue forks and dip into the fondue.

Serves 4-6

SMOKY CHEESE & HAM FONDUE

115g (4oz/1 cup) grated Gruyère cheese
225g (8oz/2 cups) grated smoked Cheddar cheese
1 tablespoon cornflour
15g (½ oz/1 tablespoon) butter
1 small onion, finely chopped
1 clove garlic, crushed
150ml (5fl oz/⅔ cup) dry white wine
½ teaspoon smoked paprika
115g (4oz) smoked ham, chopped
TO SERVE
wedges of apple
cubes of crusty bread

In a bowl, toss together the grated cheese and the cornflour.

In a saucepan, melt butter over a low heat. Add onion and garlic and cook gently for 10 minutes until softened. Place wine in the fondue pot and heat gently until bubbling. Gradually stir in grated cheeses and heat gently, stirring, until completely melted.

Stir in onion and garlic, then the paprika and ham and cook for a few more minutes until thick and smooth. Transfer the fondue pot to the lighted spirit burner. To serve, spear apple and bread on to skewers or fondue forks and dip into the fondue.

Serves 4

SOMERSET FONDUE

½ small onion
300ml (10fl oz/1¼ cups) dry cider
1 teaspoon lemon juice
450g (1lb/4 cups) grated farmhouse Cheddar cheese
1 tablespoon cornflour
2 tablespoons dry sherry
pinch mustard powder
1 teaspoon Worcestershire sauce
1 teaspoon chopped fresh sage
salt and freshly ground black pepper
TO SERVE
cubes of crusty farmhouse bread
wedges of apple
celery sticks
pickle

Rub inside of the fondue pot with cut side of onion. Place cider and lemon juice in fondue pot and heat gently until bubbling. Gradually stir in grated cheese and heat gently, stirring, until completely melted. In a small bowl, blend together cornflour and sherry. Add mustard and Worcestershire sauce. Stir into cheese mixture.

Continue to cook, stirring until thick and smooth. Stir in sage and season with salt and pepper. Transfer the fondue pot to the lighted spirit burner. To serve, spear bread on to fondue forks to dip into fondue and serve accompanied by apple, celery and pickle.

Serves 6

ITALIAN PESTO FONDUE

1 clove garlic
200ml (7fl oz/scant 1 cup) Soave wine
225g (8oz/2 cups) grated Gruyère cheese
175g (6oz/1½ cups) dolcelatte cheese, cubed
50g (2oz/½ cup) grated Parmesan cheese
1 tablespoon cornflour
2 tablespoons milk
1 tablespoon pesto sauce
salt and freshly ground black pepper
TO SERVE
foccacia and ciabatta bread cut into cubes
slices of salami
olives

Cut clove of garlic in half and rub cut side
round the inside of the fondue pot. (See
above.) Place wine in the fondue pot and
heat gently until bubbling. Gradually stir in
prepared cheeses and heat gently, stirring,
until completely melted. In a small bowl,
blend together the cornflour and milk. Stir
into the cheese mixture. Continue to cook,
stirring, until thick and smooth.

Stir in pesto and season with salt and
pepper. Transfer the fondue pot to the
lighted spirit burner. To serve, spear bread
and salami on to fondue forks to dip into
the fondue and serve accompanied by the
olives.

Serves 6

VARIATION: Instead of bread and salami,
serve cooked tortelloni to dip into the
fondue.

WELSH RAREBIT FONDUE

15g (½oz/1 tablespoon) butter
1 small onion, finely chopped
300ml (10fl oz/1½ cups) light ale
225g (8oz/2 cups) grated Caerphilly cheese
115g (4oz/1 cup) grated Welsh Cheddar cheese
1 tablespoon cornflour
2 tablespoons milk
1 teaspoon Dijon mustard
1 teaspoon Worcestershire sauce
pinch cayenne pepper
salt and freshly ground black pepper
thick slices of toast, cut into cubes, to serve

Place butter in the fondue pot and melt over a low heat.

Add onion and cook gently for 10 minutes until softened. Add light ale and heat gently until bubbling. Gradually stir in grated cheeses and heat gently, stirring, until completely melted. In a small bowl, mix together the cornflour and milk. Stir into cheese mixture.

Continue to cook, stirring, until thick and smooth. Stir in mustard, Worcestershire sauce and cayenne pepper. Season with salt and pepper. Transfer the fondue pot to the lighted spirit burner. To serve, spear cubes of toasted bread on fondue forks and dip into fondue.

Serves 4-6

MEXICAN CHILLI FONDUE

450g (1lb/4 cups) grated Monterey Jack cheese
2 tablespoons cornflour
1 clove garlic
250ml (9fl oz/generous 1 cup) Mexican lager
1 tablespoon lime juice
1-2 fresh red chillies, cored, seeded and finely chopped
salt and freshly ground black pepper
1 tablespoon chopped fresh coriander
FRIED SHALLOTS
8 shallots, thinly sliced
4 tablespoons vegetable oil
TO SERVE
pickled jalapeño chillies
tomato wedges
cubes of avocado
warm flour tortillas

Make the fried shallots. Heat oil in a frying pan, add shallots and cook, stirring, for 5 minutes or until browned. (See above.) Drain on kitchen paper and set aside. In a bowl, toss together the grated cheese and the cornflour. Cut clove of garlic in half and rub cut side round inside of the fondue pot. Add lager, lime juice and chillies and heat gently until bubbling.

Gradually stir in grated cheese and cook gently, stirring, until completely melted. Season with salt and pepper. Stir in chopped coriander and fried shallots. Transfer the fondue pot to the lighted spirit burner. Cut tortillas into strips, roll up and spear on to fondue forks to dip into the fondue, with the jalapeño chillies, tomato and avocado.

Serves 4-6

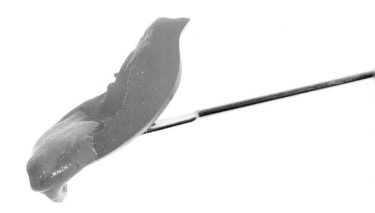

SPANISH FONDUE

1 clove garlic
250ml (9fl oz/generous 1 cup) dry Spanish white
  wine
225g (8oz/2 cups) grated Gruyère cheese
225g (8oz/2 cups) grated Manchego cheese
1 tablespoon cornflour
2 tablespoons dry sherry
2 teaspoons smoked Spanish paprika
salt and freshly ground black pepper
TO SERVE
chunks of chorizo sausage
pieces of red pepper
cubes of crusty country bread
olives
cubes of membrillo (quince paste)

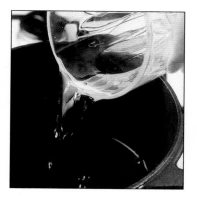

Cut clove of garlic in half and rub the cut side round inside of the fondue pot. Place wine in the fondue pot and heat gently until bubbling. (See above.) Gradually stir in the prepared cheeses and heat gently, stirring, until completely melted. In a small bowl, blend together cornflour and sherry. Stir into the cheese mixture. Continue to cook, stirring until thick and smooth.

Stir in paprika and season with salt and pepper. Transfer the fondue pot to the lighted spirit burner. To serve, spear chorizo sausage, pepper and bread on to fondue forks to dip into the fondue and serve accompanied by olives and membrillo.

Serves 4-6

CREAMY HERB & GARLIC FONDUE

1 clove garlic
150ml (5fl oz/⅔ cup) dry white wine
1 tablespoon cornflour
300ml (10fl oz/1¼ cups) crème fraîche
300g (10oz/1¼ cups) full fat soft cheese with garlic
  and herbs
pinch freshly grated nutmeg
salt and freshly ground black pepper
1 tablespoon chopped fresh chives
TO SERVE
cubes of French bread
cherry tomatoes and button mushrooms

Cut clove of garlic in half and rub the cut side round the inside of the fondue pot.

Pour 115ml (4fl oz/½ cup) of the wine into the fondue pot and heat gently until bubbling. In a small bowl, blend cornflour with the remaining wine. Add to the fondue pot and cook, stirring until thickened. Reduce the heat and add crème fraîche and soft cheese. Stir until cheese has melted.

Add nutmeg and season with salt and pepper. Sprinkle with chopped chives and transfer the fondue pot to the lighted spirit burner. To serve, spear bread, tomatoes and mushrooms on to fondue forks and dip into the fondue.

Serves 4-6

— CHILDRENS' PARTY FONDUE —

25g (1oz/2 tablespoons) butter
25g (1oz/¼ cup) plain flour
450ml (16fl oz/2 cups) milk
115g (4oz/½ cup) cream cheese
175g (6oz/1½ cups) grated Edam cheese
100ml (3½fl oz) double cream
½ teaspoon dry mustard
salt and freshly ground black pepper
TO SERVE
carrot and celery sticks
cherry tomatoes
spring onions
wedges of apple
pineapple cubes
cooked baby potatoes

Arrange vegetables and fruit on individual serving plates. Place butter in the fondue pot and heat until melted. (See above.) Stir in flour and cook, stirring for 1 minute. Gradually stir in milk, then bring to the boil and cook, stirring, until thickened and smooth. Stir in cream cheese, Edam cheese and cream. Heat gently, stirring, until cheese has melted and mixture is smooth.

Stir in mustard and season with salt and pepper. Transfer the fondue pot to the lighted spirit burner. To serve, spear vegetables and fruit on to fondue forks and dip into the fondue.

Serves 5-6

ALPINE TARTIFLETTE

butter, for greasing
350g (12oz) potatoes, scrubbed
25g (1oz/2 tablespoons) butter
1 small onion, chopped
115g (4oz) smoked bacon, cut into small pieces
1 Reblochon cheese
salt and freshly ground black pepper
5 tablespoons single cream
green salad, to serve

Preheat the oven to 220C (425F/Gas 7). Butter a gratin dish. Place scrubbed potatoes in a pan of cold water and bring to the boil.

Cook for 15-20 minutes until tender. Drain, and when cool enough to handle, peel and cut into thick slices. Meanwhile, heat butter in a frying pan. Add onion and cook for a few minutes until soft. Add bacon and cook until lightly browned. Remove onion and bacon with a slotted spoon, drain on paper towels and set aside. Add potato slices to the pan and cook for 2-3 minutes on each side, until golden.

Cut the Reblochon in half and then into cubes, leaving the crust on. Make layers of potato, bacon, onion and cheese, seasoning each layer with salt and pepper. Pour cream over the top and cook in the oven for 10-12 minutes or until the top has browned. Serve with green salad.

Serves 2

RACLETTE

1kg (2lb) small new potatoes
salt and freshly ground black pepper
450g (1lb) Raclette cheese
TO SERVE
air dried ham
salami
pickled gherkins

Scrub potatoes and place in a pan of cold salted water. Bring to the boil and cook for 10-15 minutes until tender. Drain and place in a warm serving bowl. Season with salt and pepper.

To cook the cheese, slice cheese thinly and place a layer of slices on a shallow metal tray and place under a hot grill until it starts to melt. Scrape the top melted layer of cheese off with a palette knife.

Place melted cheese on top of potatoes. Continue to cook the remaining cheese in the same way. Serve with the ham, salami and gherkins.

Serves 4

CHEESE FONDUE TARTS

425g (15oz) puff pastry
200g (7oz/1¼ cups) grated Beaufort cheese
200g (7oz/1¼ cups) grated Jarlsberg cheese
1 clove garlic, crushed
150ml (5fl oz/⅔ cup) single cream
1 tablespoon lemon juice
2 teaspoons cornflour
3 tablespoons vodka
salt and freshly ground black pepper
2 tablespoons chopped fresh chives

Preheat the oven to 220C (425F/Gas 7). On a floured surface, roll the pastry out to 3mm (⅛in) thick and cut out twelve 10cm (4in) circles.

Place circles in a 12 hole muffin tin. Prick bases and chill for 10 minutes. Press foil into pastry cases and fill with baking beans. Bake for 15-20 minutes and remove foil and beans then bake for 5 more minutes until golden.

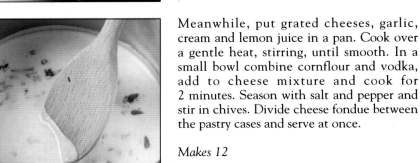

Meanwhile, put grated cheeses, garlic, cream and lemon juice in a pan. Cook over a gentle heat, stirring, until smooth. In a small bowl combine cornflour and vodka, add to cheese mixture and cook for 2 minutes. Season with salt and pepper and stir in chives. Divide cheese fondue between the pastry cases and serve at once.

Makes 12

BAKED CAMEMBERT

1 small whole Camembert cheese in its box
2 cloves garlic
2 tablespoons dry white wine (optional)
chunks of crusty bread, to serve
BACON-WRAPPED POTATOES
16 small new potatoes weighing about 450g (1lb)
salt
8 rashers streaky bacon, rinds removed
1 teaspoon Dijon mustard

Preheat the oven to 200C (400F/Gas 6).
Prepare potatoes. Scrub them and place in a
pan of salted water. Bring to the boil and
boil for 10-15 minutes until tender. Drain.

Meanwhile, remove cheese from its box and
take off the paper wrapping. Replace cheese
in the box. Peel garlic cloves and cut into
slivers. Push garlic slivers into the surface of
cheese. Drizzle wine over, if using, so that it
soaks into the holes. Replace wooden lid
and bake the cheese in the oven for 25-30
minutes until bubbling.

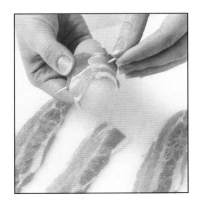

Cut each bacon rasher in half across.
Stretch out slightly with the back of a knife
and smear with a little mustard. Wrap a
piece of bacon round each potato and secure
with a cocktail stick. Grill potatoes, turning
once, until bacon is brown and crisp. Serve
cheese in its box with bacon wrapped
potatoes and crusty bread.

Serves 2-3

– CLASSIC CHOCOLATE FONDUE –

250g (9oz) plain chocolate
150ml (5fl oz/⅔ cup) double cream
2 tablespoons brandy
selection of fruit such as strawberries, pineapple,
**   banana, physallis, figs and kiwi fruit, to serve**
SPONGE FINGERS
40g (1½oz) caster sugar
1 egg
25g (1oz/½ cup) plain flour, sifted

Preheat the oven to 190C (375C/Gas 5.)
Line a baking sheet with non-stick
parchment. To make sponge fingers, place
caster sugar and egg in a large bowl.

Set bowl over a pan of barely simmering
water and whisk together until thick and
mousse-like. (See above.) Remove bowl
from heat and gently fold in flour. Using a
piping bag fitted with a 1cm (½in) plain
nozzle, pipe finger lengths of mixture on to
the prepared baking sheet. Bake for 6-8
minutes until golden. Transfer sponge
fingers to a wire rack to cool.

Break up chocolate and place in the fondue
pot with cream and brandy. Heat gently,
stirring, until chocolate has melted and
mixture is smooth. Transfer fondue pot to
the lighted spirit burner and serve with the
sponge fingers and fruit.

Serves 4-6

VARIATION: For children, substitute orange
juice for brandy.

BLACK FOREST FONDUE

400g (14oz) can stoned black cherries
150ml (5fl oz/⅔ cup) double cream
1 tablespoon kirsch
1 tablespoon cornflour
CHOCOLATE CAKE
2 eggs
115g (4oz/½ cup) softened butter
115g (4oz/½ cup) caster sugar
115g (4oz/1 cup) self-raising flour
½ teaspoon baking powder
2 tablespoons cocoa
1 tablespoon milk

Preheat the oven to 190C (375F/Gas 5).
Grease a 17.5 (7in) shallow, square tin.

To make the chocolate cake, put eggs,
butter and sugar into a bowl. (See above.)
Sift flour, baking powder and cocoa over.
Add milk and beat together until smooth.
Turn mixture into prepared tin and bake for
25 minutes until cooked and firm to the
touch. Turn on to a wire rack and leave to
cool. Cut into small squares when cold.

Empty cherries and their juice into a
blender or food processor and process until
reasonably smooth. Transfer to a fondue
pot, stir in cream and heat until simmering.
Add kirsch. In a small bowl, blend together
cornflour and 1 tablespoon of water. Add to
the fondue pot and continue to cook,
stirring, until the mixture thickens. Transfer
the fondue pot to the lighted spirit burner.
Serve with the chocolate cake to dip in.

Serves 4

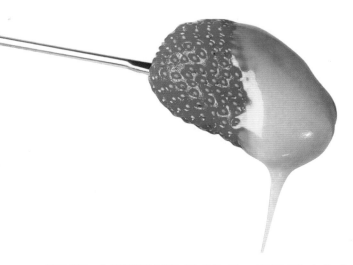

STRAWBERRY & CREAM FONDUE

50g (2oz/½ cup) strawberries
icing sugar
375g (13oz) white chocolate
225ml (8fl oz/1 cup) double cream
2 tablespoons framboise or kirsch
fresh strawberries, to serve

Place strawberries in a liquidiser or food processor and process until smooth. Press through a sieve into a bowl. Add icing sugar to taste.

Roughly chop or break up chocolate into pieces and place in the fondue pot. Add the double cream. Over a low heat, heat gently, stirring continuously, until chocolate melts. Add the framboise or kirsch, and stir until smooth.

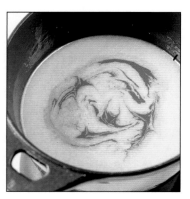

Place the fondue pot over a lighted spirit burner to keep warm. Swirl the strawberry purée on the surface of the cream sauce. Serve with fresh strawberries.

Serves 6

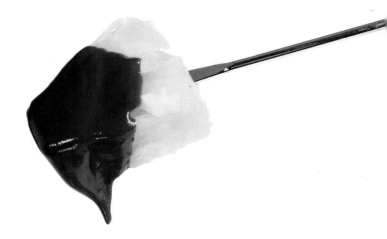

CARIBBEAN CHOCOLATE FONDUE

1 pineapple
1 mango
2 bananas
juice ½ lime
375g (13oz) good quality plain chocolate
200ml (7fl oz/scant 1 cup) coconut cream
2 tablespoons white rum
½ teaspoon freshly grated nutmeg

Cut the leafy top and the bottom off pineapple. Cut away skin and cut pineapple into quarters, lengthways. Cut out core and cut each quarter into cubes.

Peel mango then cut down on either side of stone to remove flesh. Cut into cubes. Cut bananas into slices and sprinkle with lime juice.

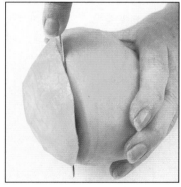

Break up chocolate into a fondue pot. Add coconut cream and heat gently on the stove, stirring, until chocolate melts. Stir in rum and nutmeg, then place over a lighted spirit burner to keep warm. Serve with the fruit.

Serves 6

-FRUITS OF THE FOREST FONDUE-

500g (1lb 2oz) packet of frozen fruits of the forest or
  summer fruits
4 tablespoons icing sugar
2 tablespoons crème de cassis or kirsch
2 tablespoons cornflour
200g (7oz/scant 1 cup) fromage frais
MINI LEMON CAKES
2 eggs
115g (4oz/½ cup) softened butter
115g (4oz/½ cup) caster sugar
115g (4oz/1 cup) self-raising flour
grated rind 1 lemon
1 tablespoon lemon juice

Preheat the oven to 190C (375F/Gas 5).
Arrange 40 paper petit four cases on a
baking sheet. (See above.) To make lemon
cakes, put eggs, butter and sugar into a bowl.
Sift flour over. Add lemon rind and juice
and beat together until smooth. Put a
teaspoon of mixture in each of the petit four
cases and bake for 10-15 minutes until
cooked and firm to the touch. Leave to cool
on a wire rack before removing from the
paper cases.

Process fruit and any juice in a blender or
food processor, then press through a sieve
into a fondue pot. Stir in icing sugar; heat
gently on the stove until almost simmering.
Blend together crème de cassis or kirsch and
cornflour and stir into fruit purée. Cook,
stirring, for 2-3 minutes until thickened.
Stir in fromage frais and heat gently,
stirring, until well blended. Transfer the
fondue pot to the lighted spirit burner and
serve fondue with lemon cakes for dipping.

Serves 6

—— BUTTERSCOTCH FONDUE ——

50g (2oz/¼ cup) unsalted butter
175g (6oz/¾ cup) demerara sugar
2 tablespoons golden syrup
½ teaspoon grated lemon rind
1 teaspoon lemon juice
2 tablespoons cornflour
400g (14oz) can evaporated milk
fresh fruit, to serve
VANILLA COOKIES
1 vanilla pod
115g (4oz/½ cup) unsalted butter
85g (3oz/⅓ cup) caster sugar
1 egg yolk
150g (5oz/1 cup) self-raising flour

To make the cookies, slit vanilla pod lengthways and scrape black seeds into a large bowl. (See above.) Add butter and sugar and beat together until light and fluffy. Beat in egg yolk, then stir in flour to make a stiff dough. Wrap dough in clear film and chill for 15 minutes. Preheat the oven to 190C (375F/Gas 5). Grease 2 or 3 baking sheets. Divide dough into 30 small balls and place well apart on baking sheets. Flatten slightly. Bake for 15 minutes until golden brown. Transfer to wire racks to cool.

To make fondue, place butter, sugar, syrup, lemon rind and juice in a fondue pot and heat gently until sugar has dissolved. Boil for 1 minute. Blend cornflour and 2 tablespoons of the evaporated milk. Stir remaining evaporated milk into sugar mixture. Heat until just simmering then simmer for 2-3 minutes. Stir in blended cornflour then bring to the boil, stirring, until smooth and thick. Transfer to the lighted spirit burner and serve with the cookies and fruit.

Serves 6

BANOFFEE FONDUE

250g (9oz) vanilla fudge
300ml (10fl oz/1¼ cup) double cream
sliced bananas, to serve
MINI CHOCOLATE MUFFINS
40g (1½oz) plain chocolate
150g (5oz/1¼ cups) plain flour
1½ teaspoons baking powder
pinch salt
½ teaspoon ground cinnamon
50g (2oz/¼ cup) caster sugar
1 egg
115ml (4fl oz/½ cup) milk
50g (2oz/¼ cup) butter, melted and cooled slightly

Preheat the oven to 400F (200C).

Arrange 20 petit-four cases on a baking sheet. To make the muffins, chop the chocolate into small pieces. Sift the flour, baking powder, salt and cinnamon into a bowl. In another bowl, whisk together the sugar, egg, milk and melted butter. Add the dry ingredients and the chocolate and fold together quickly and lightly until just combined. Divide the mixture between the petit-four cases and bake in the oven for 15 minutes or until well risen and golden. Transfer to a wire rack to cool.

To make the fondue, place the fudge and cream in the fondue pot and heat gently, stirring until melted and smooth. Transfer the fondue pot to the lighted burner. To serve, spear the banana and muffin cakes on to bamboo skewers or fondue forks.

Serves 6

─── SPICED APRICOT FONDUE ───

2 x 400g (14oz) cans apricot halves in natural juice
1 sachet wine mulling spices
2 tablespoons cornflour
300g (10oz/1¼ cups) fromage frais
kiwi fruit, to serve
ALMOND MACAROONS
2 large egg whites
85g (3oz/¼ cup) ground almonds
115g (4oz/½ cup) caster sugar
1 tablespoon cornflour
few drops almond essence
24 split blanched almonds

Preheat the oven to 190C (375F/Gas 5). Line 2 or 3 baking sheets with non-stick paper.

Make the macaroons. Reserve 2 teaspoons of egg white for brushing. In a large bowl, whisk remaining egg whites until frothy. (See above.) Stir in ground almonds, sugar, cornflour and almond essence. Mix together thoroughly. Place 24 small spoonfuls of mixture on to lined baking sheets. Smooth out slightly with the back of a spoon. Place a split blanched almond in centre of each macaroon and brush the top with reserved egg white. Bake for 10-15 minutes until a pale golden brown. Leave for 5 minutes then transfer to a wire rack to cool.

Place apricots and juice in fondue pot with spice sachet. Heat until simmering then remove from heat and leave to cool. Remove sachet and place apricots and juice in a blender or food processor. Process to a purée and return to fondue pot. Reheat gently. In a small bowl, blend cornflour with a little water. Add to apricot purée and continue to heat, stirring, until thickened. Stir in fromage frais then transfer fondue pot to lighted burner. Serve with kiwi fruit and macaroons.

Serves 4-6

— LEMON MERINGUE FONDUE —

4 tablespoons cornflour
400ml (14fl oz/1¾ cups) coconut milk
grated rind and juice 2 lemons
50g (2oz/¼ cup) caster sugar
pieces of mango, to serve
MERINGUES
2 egg whites
115g (4oz/½ cup) caster sugar
½ teaspoon vanilla extract

Preheat the oven to 110C (225F/Gas¼).
Line 2 or 3 baking sheets with non-stick
paper. Put egg whites in a large clean bowl
and whisk until meringue holds soft peaks.

Add sugar, 1 tablespoonful at a time,
whisking well after each addition. Continue
whisking until stiff and glossy. Fold in
vanilla with a rubber spatula. Put 24
teaspoonfuls of mixture on to lined baking
sheets. Bake for 1-1½ hours until dry and
crisp. Turn off oven and leave meringues in
oven to cool. Remove from the paper when
cool.

To make the fondue, put cornflour and a
little of the coconut milk in the fondue pot
and stir to make a paste. Stir in remaining
coconut milk. Bring to the boil on top of
the stove, stirring, and continue to cook for
2-3 minutes until thickened. Remove from
heat and add lemon rind and juice and
sugar. Reheat then transfer the fondue pot
to the lighted spirit burner. Serve with the
mango and meringues.

Serves 4-6

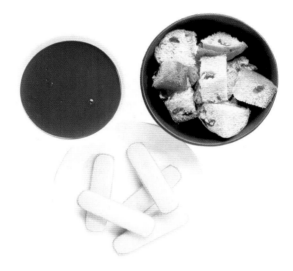

TIRAMISU FONDUE

250g (9oz) mascarpone cheese
2 tablespoons rum
100g (3½oz) plain chocolate
1 tablespoon coffee granules
1 tablespoon caster sugar (optional)
TO SERVE
squares of panettone
Italian sponge finger biscuits
strawberries

Place mascarpone cheese in the fondue pot with the rum. Heat gently on top of the stove, stirring, until mascarpone melts.

Break up chocolate into small pieces and add to the fondue pot. Continue to heat gently until chocolate melts.

Add coffee granules and stir until mixture is smooth. Taste the fondue and add sugar if desired. Transfer the fondue pot to the lighted spirit burner and serve with panettone, sponge fingers and strawberries.

Serves 4

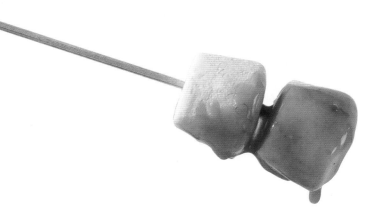

MARSHMALLOW FONDUE

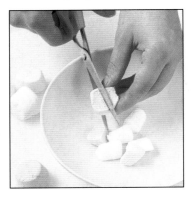

225g (8oz) marshmallows
150ml (5fl oz/⅔ cup) bottled raspberry or
  strawberry coulis
150ml (5fl oz/⅔ cup) double cream
1-2 tablespoons lemon juice (optional)
TO SERVE
marshmallows
sponge fingers
strawberries

Using wet scissors, snip marshmallows into
pieces and place in the fondue pot.

Add fruit coulis and cream. Place over a
very low heat and cook gently, stirring, until
marshmallows have melted and mixture is
smooth.

Add lemon juice, to taste, if desired.
Transfer the fondue pot to the lighted spirit
burner and serve with marshmallows,
sponge fingers and strawberries.

Serves 4

– BANANA & CHOCOLATE BITES –

6 firm ripe bananas
115g (4oz/¾ cup) shelled pistachio nuts
225g (8oz) plain chocolate
4 tablespoons single cream

Peel bananas and cut them into 2.5cm (1in) lengths. Cover a metal baking sheet with clear film.

Arrange banana slices in a single layer on the baking sheet and place in the freezer. Leave in the freezer for at least 3 hours or until completely frozen. Coarsely chop pistachio nuts and divide between 4 small shallow dishes. When ready to serve, break up chocolate into the fondue pot. Add cream and heat gently on top of the stove, stirring, until chocolate is melted and mixture is smooth.

Transfer fondue pot to the lighted spirit burner. Bring banana pieces to the table on the metal baking sheet. To serve, spear the banana on to bamboo skewers or fondue forks, dip into the chocolate and then into the chopped nuts.

Serves 6

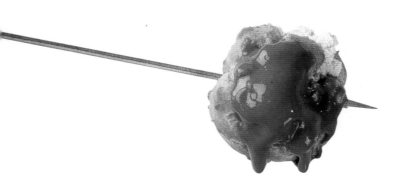

– CHOCOLATE ORANGE FONDUE –

350g (12oz) plain chocolate chips
4 tablespoons double cream
50ml (2fl oz/¼ cup) orange juice
1 teaspoon grated orange rind
PROFITEROLES
50g (2oz/¼ cup) butter
70g (2½oz) plain flour, sifted
2 eggs, lightly beaten
150ml (5fl oz/⅔ cup) double cream, whipped

Preheat the oven to 220C (425F/Gas 7). Butter 2 baking sheets. Make the profiteroles, place butter in a pan with 150ml (5fl oz/ ⅔ cup) water. Bring just to the boil and remove from the heat.

Add flour to pan, stirring constantly with a wooden spoon, until combined. (See above.) Return pan to heat and continue beating over a low heat until mixture is smooth and pulls away from sides of the pan. Remove from heat and leave to cool for a minute. Beat in eggs, a little at a time, until mixture is smooth and glossy. Using 2 spoons, place 24 walnut-sized mounds of mixture well apart on the baking sheets. Bake for 20 minutes until well risen and golden brown. Reduce oven temperature to 180C (350F/Gas 4). Make a hole in each bun.

Return buns to the oven for 5 minutes. Cool on a wire rack. Spoon a little cream into each bun. Place chocolate chips, cream and orange juice in a large microwave safe bowl. Cover and microwave at full power for 1 minute. Stir until smooth. Heat for a few more seconds, if necessary, until all the chocolate is melted. Stir in orange rind. Transfer to a fondue pot and place on a lighted burner. Spear profiteroles on to bamboo skewers or fondue forks, to serve.

Serves 4-6

CAPPUCINO FONDUE

225g (8oz) white chocolate
50ml (2fl oz/¼ cup) strong espresso coffee
150ml (5fl oz/⅔ cup) double cream
drinking chocolate, for sprinkling
PISTACHIO BISCOTTI
225g (8oz/2 cups) plain flour
1 teaspoon baking powder
pinch salt
175g (6oz/¾ cup) caster sugar
2 eggs
grated rind 1 lemon
1 tablespoon lemon juice
115g (4oz/¾ cup) blanched almonds, toasted and
    roughly chopped
50g (2oz/⅓ cup) shelled pistachio nuts, roughly
    chopped

Preheat the oven to 180C (350F/Gas 4).
Line a baking sheet with non-stick
parchment. To make biscotti, sift flour,
baking powder and salt into a mixing bowl.
Stir in sugar, eggs, lemon rind and juice and
nuts. Mix together to form a firm dough. (See
above.) Roll dough into a ball, cut in half
and roll each portion into a roll about 3cm
(1¼in) in diameter. Place rolls on the baking
sheet at least 8cm (3½in) apart. Lightly
flatten rolls and bake for 15-20 minutes until
golden brown. Remove from oven and leave
to cool and firm up for 5 minutes.

With a serrated knife, cut biscotti at an
angle into 1cm (½in) thick slices. Arrange
slices on baking sheet and return to the
oven for a further 15 minutes, turning once.
Transfer to a wire rack to cool. To make the
fondue, place chocolate, coffee and cream in
the fondue pot and heat gently on top of the
stove until chocolate has melted and
mixture is smooth. Sprinkle with drinking
chocolate then transfer to the lighted spirit
burner and serve with the biscotti.

Serves 4

- CHOCOLATE & HONEY FONDUE -

300g (10oz) plain chocolate
1 heaped tablespoon honey
300ml (10fl oz/1¼ cups) double cream
SPICED FRUIT
400g (14oz) ready-to-eat dried fruit such as apricots
  and prunes
1 cinnamon stick
1 star anise
4 cloves
1 tablespoon honey

To prepare the fruit, place in a saucepan
and cover with water. Add cinnamon stick,
star anise and cloves, and bring to the boil.

Stir in honey and remove from the heat. Set
aside and leave until cold. Drain fruit and
pat dry on paper towels. Arrange on
6 individual plates.

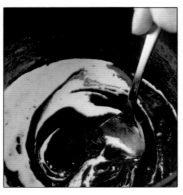

Break up the chocolate and place in the
fondue pot with honey and cream. Heat
gently, stirring, until chocolate has melted
and mixture is smooth. Transfer the fondue
pot to the lighted spirit burner and serve
with the fruit.

Serves 6

NOTE: For both the fondue and fruit, choose
a fragrant blossom honey such as Mexican
wildflower honey.

– RHUBARB & CUSTARD FONDUE –

550g (1¼lb) cans rhubarb in syrup
450g (1lb) carton ready-made fresh custard
GINGER SPONGE
2 eggs
115g (4oz/½ cup) softened butter
115g (4oz/½ cup) golden caster sugar
115g (4oz/1 cup) self-raising flour
1 teaspoon ground ginger
pinch baking powder
2 pieces ginger from a jar of stem ginger in syrup,
  finely chopped
1 tablespoon syrup from the ginger jar

Preheat oven to 180C (350F/Gas 4). Grease
a 17.5cm (7in) shallow, square cake tin.

To make the ginger sponge, put eggs, butter
and caster sugar in a bowl. Sift flour, ginger
and baking powder into the bowl. Add
chopped ginger and syrup and beat together
until thoroughly blended. (See above.)
Turn the mixture into the prepared tin and
bake for 25 minutes or until golden and firm
to the touch. Leave in the tin for 5 minutes
then turn out on to a wire rack to cool. Cut
into small squares when cold.

To make the fondue, drain rhubarb and
place in a blender or food processor. Process
to a purée then place in the fondue pot with
the custard. Heat on top of the stove until
hot but not boiling. Transfer the fondue pot
to the lighted spirit burner and serve with
the ginger sponge.

Serves 4-6

ROUILLE

2 slices white bread, crusts removed
2 red peppers, seeded and quartered
2 fresh red chillies, seeded and chopped
2 cloves garlic, crushed
olive oil

Place bread in a shallow dish with 3-4 tablespoons cold water and soak for 10 minutes.

Grill red pepper quarters, skin side up, until the skin is charred and blistered. Place in a plastic bag until cool enough to handle. Peel off skins and chop flesh roughly.

Place red pepper flesh in a blender or food processor. Drain the bread and squeeze out the excess moisture. Add to peppers with chillies and garlic. Process to a coarse paste then gradually add enough olive oil to give the desired consistency. Transfer to small serving bowls.

Serves 4-6

CHILLI TOMATO SAUCE

1 onion
2 sticks celery
1 clove garlic
1 red pepper
1 red chilli
2 tablespoons oil
400g (14oz) canned chopped tomatoes
1 teaspoon molasses or soft brown sugar
salt and freshly ground black pepper
chopped fresh coriander, to garnish

Finely chop the onion and sticks celery. Crush garlic and seed red pepper and chop. Core and seed the chilli and chop very finely.

Heat oil in a saucepan. Add onion, celery, garlic and red pepper and cook for 10 minutes until soft. Add chilli, tomatoes and molasses and season with salt and pepper.

Bring to the boil, cover and simmer gently for 20-30 minutes until thickened and well blended. Garnish with chopped coriander.

Serves 4-6

—— TWO MAYONNAISES ——

SAFFRON MAYONNAISE:
150ml (5fl oz/⅔ cup) fish stock
½ teaspoon saffron strands
150ml (5fl oz/⅔ cup) mayonnaise
1 teaspoon lemon juice
salt and freshly ground black pepper
AIOLI:
150ml (5fl oz/⅔ cup) mayonnaise
2 cloves garlic, crushed
1 teaspoon Dijon mustard
salt and freshly ground black pepper (optional)

To make the saffron mayonnaise, put fish stock in a saucepan and bring to the boil.

Boil until reduced to 1 tablespoon. Add saffron strands and leave to cool. Strain stock into a bowl and stir in mayonnaise. Add lemon juice and season with salt and pepper. (Salt will not be needed if the fish stock was salty.) Spoon into a serving bowl, cover and chill until required.

To make the aioli, place mayonnaise, garlic and mustard in a bowl. Mix together and season with salt and pepper, if desired. Transfer to a serving bowl, cover and chill until required. Set aside.

Serves 4

CUMBERLAND SAUCE

1 shallot
1 orange
1 lemon
115g (4oz/⅓ cup) redcurrant jelly
1 teaspoon Dijon mustard
70ml (2½ fl oz/⅓ cup) port
1 teaspoon arrowroot

Chop shallot very finely and place in a saucepan. With a peeler, remove the rind of orange and lemon.

Cut into very fine strips and add to the pan. Cover with cold water, bring to the boil and cook for 5 minutes. Drain and set aside. Meanwhile, halve orange and lemon and squeeze juice. Set aside. Add redcurrant jelly to the pan and heat gently, stirring until melted.

Stir in mustard, port, juice of orange and lemon and blanched rind and shallot. Cook for about 5 minutes. In a small bowl, mix arrowroot to a paste with a 1 tablespoon of cold water. Add to the sauce in the pan. Simmer for a further 2-3 minutes until slightly thickened then leave to cool before serving.

Serves 4

TOMATO & OLIVE SALSA

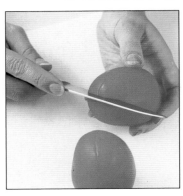

4 plum tomatoes
175g (6oz/1¼ cups) mixed pitted green and black
  olives, roughly chopped
1 small red onion, finely chopped
1 fresh red chilli, cored, seeded and finely chopped
2 tablespoons olive oil
salt and freshly ground black pepper

To peel the tomatoes, cut a cross in the
rounded side of each tomato.

Place them in a bowl and pour boiling water
over to cover. Leave for 1 minute then drain
and cover with cold water. Leave for 1 more
minute, then remove and peel. Cut
tomatoes into quarters and remove cores,
then cut tomato flesh into tiny dice and
place in a bowl.

Add olives, onion and chilli to tomatoes in
the bowl. Stir in olive oil and season with
salt and pepper. Transfer to a serving bowl
and serve.

Serves 4

— AVOCADO & MELON SALSA —

1 ripe avocado
½ canteloupe melon
juice 1 lime
4 spring onions, very finely chopped
1 fresh red chilli, cored, seeded and very finely
   chopped
salt and freshly ground black pepper
mint leaves, to garnish

Cut the avocado in half. Remove the stone
and peel off the skin.

Remove seeds from melon and cut away
skin. Cut avocado and melon into small
dice and place in a bowl with lime juice.
Toss together well. Add spring onions and
chilli. Season with salt and pepper.

Cover closely with clear film and leave to
stand for 30 minutes. (Do not leave for
longer than this or the avocado will
discolour.) Transfer to a serving dish.
Roughly tear or chop the mint leaves and
scatter over the salsa before serving.

Serves 4

VARIATION: Any type of melon can be used
as long as it is ripe and has a good flavour.
You should have 225g (8oz) melon after
peeling and seeding.

——— BEAN SALAD ———

400g (14oz) canned black-eyed beans
400g (14oz) canned red kidney beans
4 sticks celery, chopped
1 green pepper, seeded and roughly chopped
1 small red onion, finely chopped
4 tablespoons olive oil
1 tablespoon lime juice
1 teaspoon sugar
½-1 teaspoon hot pepper sauce
salt and freshly ground black pepper
2 tablespoons chopped fresh parsley

Drain and rinse black-eyed beans and red kidney beans. Place in a bowl.

Add the celery, green pepper and onion to the beans.

In a bowl, mix together olive oil, lime juice, sugar and hot pepper sauce. Season with salt and pepper. Pour over the bean mixture and mix well. Set aside for 30 minutes then transfer to a serving dish. Scatter with chopped parsley and serve.

Serves 4-6

VARIATIONS: The combination of beans can be varied according to preference and what is available.

COUSCOUS SALAD

3 tablespoons olive oil
5 spring onions, chopped
1 clove garlic, crushed
1 teaspoon ground cumin
350ml (12fl oz/1½ cups) vegetable stock
175g (6oz/1 cup) couscous
2 tomatoes, peeled and chopped
4 tablespoons chopped fresh parsley
4 tablespoons chopped fresh mint
1 fresh green chilli, cored, seeded and finely chopped
2 tablespoons lemon juice
salt and freshly ground black pepper
toasted pine nuts and grated lemon rind, to garnish

Heat oil in a saucepan. Add spring onions and garlic.

Stir in cumin. Add stock and bring to the boil. Remove the pan from the heat and stir in couscous. Leave to stand for 10 minutes until couscous has absorbed all the liquid. Fluff up with a fork and transfer to a serving dish.

Leave to cool then stir in tomatoes, parsley, mint, chilli and lemon juice. Season with salt and pepper. Leave to stand for up to 1 hour to allow the flavours to develop. Scatter pine nuts and lemon rind over and serve.

Serves 4

– ORANGE & RED ONION SALAD –

6 oranges
2 small red onions
1 tablespoon cumin seeds
1 teaspoon coarsely ground black pepper
1 tablespoon chopped fresh mint
6 tablespoons olive oil
salt
mint sprigs and black olives, to garnish

Working over a bowl to catch the juice, cut the skin away from oranges, removing the pith.

With a sharp knife, slice the oranges thinly. Slice onions across thinly, into rings, then separate the layers of the rings. Arrange the orange and onion slices in layers in a shallow dish. Sprinkle each layer with cumin seeds, black pepper, mint, olive oil and salt to taste.

Pour any orange juice saved from slicing oranges over the salad. Leave in a cool place for about 2 hours, for the flavours to develop. Just before serving, scatter the salad with mint sprigs and black olives.

Serves 6

VARIATION: Slices of fennel may be added to this salad.

ORIENTAL GREEN SALAD

115g (4oz) mange-tout, trimmed and halved
1 small head Chinese leaves
8 spring onions, roughly chopped
1 green pepper, seeded and sliced
½ small cucumber
115g (4oz/2 cups) beansprouts
2 tablespoons chopped roasted cashew nuts, and
  2 tablespoons chopped fresh coriander, to garnish
DRESSING:
2.5cm (1in) piece fresh root ginger, grated
1 clove garlic, crushed
1 fresh red chilli, cored, seeded and finely chopped
1 teaspoon clear honey
grated rind and juice 1 lime
2 tablespoons oil
1 tablespoon soy sauce

Bring a pan of water to the boil, add mange-tout, cook for 2 minutes then drain and refresh in cold water. (See above.) Drain again and place in a bowl. Finely shred Chinese leaves and add to the bowl with the spring onions and green pepper.

Peel cucumber, cut in half lengthways and slice thinly. Add to the bowl with beansprouts. To make the dressing, whisk together ginger, garlic, chilli, honey, lime rind and juice, oil and soy sauce. Pour over the salad and mix well. Transfer to a serving bowl. Before serving, scatter over chopped cashew nuts and coriander.

Serves 4-6

INDEX